D1556599

Acknowledgement to Austin MacCormick

For over a quarter of a century prison men and women,
borrowing from one of their revered leaders, Austin MacCormick,
have been saying, "If only I had the right staff, I could
run a good prison in an old red barn."

This is a book about recently built institutions, the
new red barns, in which good and dedicated people are
operating their correctional programs.

Acknowledgement to LEAA

This book was written during the period when the
author served as a member of the Task Force on
Corrections of the National Advisory Commission on
Criminal Justice Standards and Goals of the Law
Enforcement Assistance Administration, United States
Department of Justice. He was assigned the task of
drafting the chapter on major institutions for that
task force. Some material in this book has been
included, in modified form, in the report of that task force.

To Nellie Lee Bok

The New Red Barn:

A Critical Look
at the Modern
American Prison

William G. Nagel

Published for The American Foundation, Incorporated
Institute of Corrections, Philadelphia, Pennsylvania
by Walker and Company, New York, New York 10019

Copyright, ©, 1973,
by The American
Foundation, Incorporated

All rights reserved.
No part of this book
in excess of three hundred words
may be reproduced in any form
without permission in writing
from the publisher.

Library of Congress
Catalog Card No. 72-95803
ISBN 0-8027-0423-9

Contents

The New Red Barn:

A Critical Look
at the Modern
American Prison

Preface

Over the years different civilizations have defined criminal behavior in a variety of ways, and have used a variety of methods to control it. These methods have included execution, exile, slavery, mutilation, imprisonment, flogging, fines, probation, parole, and others – both baneful and benign.

This book is about one of these methods – imprisonment – and especially about the physical plants in which imprisonment takes place. It is the product of a study made by The American Foundation's Institute of Corrections, and undertaken at the specific request of the Law Enforcement Assistance Administration (LEAA) of the United States Department of Justice.

The LEAA had a very practical reason for wanting an evaluation of America's correctional facilities. Congress passed legislation in 1970 that authorized large federal expenditures for state and local prison construction. The LEAA was to administer these funds and wanted guidance as to the "good" and the "bad" of contemporary correctional architecture.

The American Foundation, Incorporated, is a privately endowed nonprofit organization founded in 1924 by Edward Bok. Since its inception it has worked, within the law, at its founder's purpose – to help make representative government more responsive to the needs of people. During the last decade corrections – which is a responsibility of representative government – has been the major social interest of the Institute of Corrections, one division of the foundation. The institute and its staff have devoted considerable attention over the years to the design of correctional facilities. The board of the foundation was eager, therefore, to accept the LEAA's invitation and decided to do all the research and field work at no cost to the government. In this way the judgments of the researchers were spared any unconscious biases which might develop when studies are publicly financed.

To staff the study the foundation assembled a multidisciplinary team composed of a correctional administrator, architects, psychologists, social scientists, and secretaries. The members of the team are identified elsewhere in this volume.

A total of over 100 correctional institutions were visited throughout the country. Most of them were new because our interest was in the current state of the art. Included were 38 prisons, 19 jails, 6 reformatories, 13 community correctional centers, and 25 facilities serving delinquent juveniles. They were located in 26 states.

The primary research method was direct observation and on-site evaluation. The many field trips were usually made by three members of the research team—the correctional administrator, an architect, and a psychologist. The basic procedure was a walking tour of the institution, usually with complete freedom to speak with inmates and staff individually and in groups. Every possible attempt was made to observe the housing, treatment, and work situations of the inmates. Simultaneous impressions were noted of the overall effect of the physical structure and its location on staff, inmates, and program. All observations were carefully recorded and subsequently analyzed.

Architectural plans for the many institutions were acquired and studied. Thousands of photographs were taken. We also studied proposed plans of institutions yet to be built.

The research team received enormous support and assistance from a multitude of people. They include the members of the foundation's board and its President, Nellie Lee Bok, who gave us complete freedom and generous financial support; the Ad Hoc Committee on Correctional Architecture; dozens of architects who shared their plans and thoughts with us; scores of correctional administrators who opened their doors and minds to our searching inquiries; hundreds of inmates who gave us many candid thoughts; John Conrad, Lawrence Carpenter, Milton Rector, Austin MacCormick, Fred Moyer, Richard W. Velde, and Robert Kutak, some of whom read much of the draft, criticized it, and helped to improve it; Edith E. Flynn who contributed to the evolution of my thought during these past two years and especially to my comprehension of total systems planning; Albert G. Fraser, corrections' grandest old man who, at 95, read much of this in its draft form and who always pricked any inflated ideas I might allow myself as to the value of this effort; and Ethel M. Nagel who understands both Nagelese and English and diligently translated the text from the latter to the former.

William G. Nagel
Yardley, Pennsylvania
March 1973

Background

Early in 1971 three of us—an architect, a psychologist, and myself—began to travel around the country to look at over 100 of America's newer correctional institutions. We had been asked to do this by the Law Enforcement Assistance Administration of the United States Department of Justice, because that agency was being mandated by Congress to help fund, for the first time, state and local correctional construction.

The Background of Corrections

Before we began our many trips which eventually took us into 26 states we took a journey back through history. One of our main guides was Norman Johnston who has almost made a career of studying the old prisons of the world. He wrote a monograph for us which has been published as a companion piece to this volume. Called *The Human Cage*, it is a brief and fascinating history of prison architecture.

Our journeys were trips that very few people can take. This book which will describe the contemporary correctional institutions and programs that we saw will begin, therefore, with a brief summary of our journey into history. It will end with our recommendations for the future.

Imprisonment as the primary means of enforcing the customs, mores, or laws of a people is a relatively modern device. In earlier times restitution, exile, and a variety of methods of corporal and capital punishment, many of them unspeakably barbarous, were utilized. Confinement, when it was used at all, was for detention only. In fact, Roman law decreed confinement to be illegal as punishment. Similarly, the earliest English law viewed confinement only as a way of holding a person who could not give security.

It appears that the church was the first institution to authorize confinement as punishment, rather than mere trial detention. In preparing his book Dr. Johnston searched for the antecedents of the philosophy of imprisonment as well as the architecture which came to be associated with it. He describes these antecedents as follows:

> *The concept of imprisonment as a substitute for death or mutilation of the body was derived in part from a custom of the early church of granting asylum or sanctuary to fugitives and criminals. Begun largely during the reign of Constantine, this ancient right existed earlier among Assyrians, Hebrews, and others. The church at that time had under its aegis a large number of clergy, clerks, functionaries, monks and serfs, and, except the latter, most of these fell under the jurisdiction of the church courts. Traditionally forbidden to shed blood and drawing on the Christian theme of purification through suffering, these canon courts came to subject the wrongdoer to reclusion and even solitary cellular confinement, not as punishment alone, but as a way of providing conditions under which penitence would most likely occur.*
>
> *...Some of the monastic quarters provided totally separate facilities for each monk so that it was a simple matter to lock up an errant brother for brief periods.*

As "mother houses" of monastic orders had satellite houses often located in less desirable places, it was also the practice to transfer monks for periods of time to such locations. There is some evidence that some of these satellites came to be regarded as punitive facilities.

Dr. Johnston points out that the order of Cluny, for example, built very unpleasant facilities, the cells of which were without doors or windows, and sometimes prisoners were kept there in irons. Light, heat, or wine were seldom provided. Aside from the monastic prisons, such as that of the order of Cluny, every seat of church government, episcopal palace and the like, contained prisons. One of the most famous structures in France is Mont St. Michel, which has served successively as an ecclesiastical, civil, and military prison.

During the Inquisition a third type of ecclesiastical prison was built. In some of these, certain heretics, having been spared death, were imprisoned for life, often in single rooms underground. During this period, for instance, a Portuguese religious prison was built that contained cells for witches, sorcerers, and sinners.

The church played still another role in the creation of a system of confinement facilities which became antecedents of our jails and prison system. With the breakup of feudalism there followed a period of extreme unrest throughout all of Europe. The serf, no longer tied to the land or needed on the land, began to move around the countryside and into the city, where he seldom was able to find remunerative employment. As a vagrant he became involved in all sorts of petty and serious criminal activity.

Church people, exhibiting a new humanitarianism, tried to find acceptable alternatives to transportation and the harsh corporal and capital punishments prevalent at the time. Their invention was the "workhouse." This ingenious device proposed to serve two vital purposes. It would take vagabonds, beggars and petty thieves off the streets and at the same time it would introduce them to the work ethic.

Workhouses were built all over Europe, and soon became filled with petty offenders of various sexes and ages whose crimes seemed too trivial to warrant the block, the gallows, or the various forms of corporal punishment that twisted minds had invented.

The Birth of the Penitentiary — An American Creation

In colonial America, the extensive use of physical punishment was a legacy from our European ancestors. Concepts of sin and the consequent need for expiation were blended into a strict criminal code which was exacting in its demands and terrible in its toll. In general, the colonial penal system emphasized revenge and employed the severest measures to deter potential criminals. There were in colonial America no actual penal institutions as we have come to know them, because the practice of "sentencing" convicted criminals to serve time in an institution was then unknown.

In some colonies, however, there were workhouses for debtors and "gaols" for untried criminals. Conditions in these gaols were horrendous. The indiscriminate mixing of criminals with the insane, the young with the old, men with women—and all at the mercy of gaol-keepers who ran the gaols for profit—all insured a hellish existence for the incarcerated. It was not uncommon for prisoners to be forced to beg for food from people passing by. Food, liquor, and general necessities were available to those who had the means to purchase them. The sustenance of those who were poor was left to the mercy or whim of the gaoler. Records indicate that prisoners actually starved to death in Pennsylvania.

After the Revolutionary War was fought and won, some states of the new nation began seeking new methods for the disposition of criminals. The manner of handling convicted offenders was in extreme need of reform and nowhere was reform more likely to occur than in Pennsylvania. In that state in the period immediately following the Revolution, there converged several significant forces which were to change the course of penal matters in America and indeed throughout the world. That the severe criminal codes imposed upon them during their colonial status were distasteful to the Quakers and other humanists became evident as early as 1776. In that year, in the frame of the provisional state constitution they wrote: "The Penal Laws heretofore used shall be reformed by the future legislature of the State, as soon as may be, and punishments made in some cases less sanguinary, and in general more proportionate to the crimes."

The widespread use of corporal punishment was especially abrasive to the religious sensibilities of that state's inhabitants, a good number of whom were Quakers. In addition, the desire of the new country to divest itself of England's mores was strong. There was also an intellectual movement afoot which fundamentally altered man's views of himself and society. Democracy won out over Old World ways. Man could rule himself. No longer was it deemed necessary to respond to criminal behavior by repression and force only.

The wretched conditions of those held in the early gaols were quite visible, because prisoners were used in public works. The original tasks assigned to these inmates were largely heavy manual labor such as the leveling and grading of roads, digging ditches, and filling up ponds. To prevent escapes and attacks upon the jeering public, who viewed the situation as a sport, the prisoners "were encumbered with iron collars and chains, to which bombshells were attached, to be dragged along while they performed their degrading service, under the eye of keepers armed with swords, blunderbusses, and other weapons of destruction."

In analyzing the influences on the reform of the early American penal apparatus, Dr. Harry Elmer Barnes cites two factors. The first is the general force of progress based on the spreading philosophy of rationalism. The main tenet was "the firm conviction that social progress and advancement was possible through sweeping social reforms carried out according to the dictates of 'pure reason.'" It is Barnes' further contention that "so barbarous and archaic a part of the old order as the current criminal jurisprudence and penal administration of the time could not long remain immune to the growing spirit of progress and enlightenment."

Another social historian, Alice Felt Tyler, concurs with the inevitability of penal reform in the fledgling country. She points to the philosophical incompatibility of such a primitive penal system in a nation so committed to the perfectability of its people: "If American statesmen were to give more than lip service to the humane and optimistic idea of man's improvability, they must remove the barbarism and vindictiveness from their penal codes and admit that one great objective of punishment for crime must be the reformation of the criminal."

Another propelling force behind penal reform in the newly independent Pennsylvania was a small group of concerned individuals who translated the growing feeling of enlightened humanitarianism into a concerted effort toward a specific goal — the reformation of the penal structure. In 1787 this group adopted the worthy title of "The Philadelphia Society for Alleviating the Miseries of Public Prisons." One hundred years later, the Society's membership shortened the title to "The Pennsylvania Prison Society." Under the same name it is still, 185 years after its founding, a force for penal reform.

A person of no less importance than Dr. Benjamin Rush lent his prominence to the Prison Society. During the year of its inception he began writing documents intended to persuade the legislature of Pennsylvania to repeal the law requiring degrading public work. Instead, "more private or even solitary labour" was to be required.

Other early recommendations of the Prison Society included separation of hardened criminals from first offenders, segregation of the sexes, and the prohibition of liquor sales in the gaols. Basically, these recommendations contain the nucleus of what was to become known as the Pennsylvania System of prison discipline. The recommendations are significant in that they are the germ of the original "prison program" and are based on certain assumptions about behavior and what might be done to modify it. The authors of one particular document presented to the Pennsylvania General Assembly on January 9, 1788, state specifically the underlying reasons for their suggestions: solitary labor because "it might be conducted more steadily and uniformly"; separation of young from hardened prisoners because "the evils of familiarizing young minds to vicious characters would be removed"; segregation of the sexes and prohibition of liquor because these "prevent the useful reflections which might be produced by solitary labour and strict temperance."

In March of 1789, the Supreme Executive Council of the Commonwealth accepted the main recommendations of the Prison Society. The General Assembly enacted subsequent legislation, and out of it was born the penitentiary system.

The immediate effect of the legislation was the renovation of the Walnut Street Jail in Philadelphia to include a "cellhouse" for the confinement of prisoners who were considered hardened and therefore of potentially bad effect on the others. The dimensions of the cells were specified to be 6 feet by 8 feet by 9 feet. They were to be constructed in such a manner that virtual isolation was imposed on the inhabitants and communication with other prisoners was impossible.

In addition to the architectural modification, changes wrought by these laws extended beyond the physical structure of the jail. Indeed, there seems to have occurred a purge of all conditions against which the Prison Society railed in its writings. The sale and consumption of liquor was terminated. There was complete segregation of the sexes. Debtors were put into quarters separate from convicted felons. Children were not housed in the jail. Food and clothing were supplied to prisoners at the expense of the commonwealth. The days of licentiousness and debauchery, of starvation and nakedness in the cold jails were to be no more. Significantly, the legislature and the Prison Society drew up rules which were "the first ever compiled in this country for the operation of a penal institution."

In 1829 legislation was passed providing for solitary confinement as the state's official penal policy. To accomplish that end, Eastern State Penitentiary was built in Philadelphia. This event marked the birth of more than an institution. Indeed, an entire system of corrections came into being. The Pennsylvania System, as it came to be known, was based on the concept of solitary confinement whereby convicted prisoners were to be taken from the community and kept in cells isolated from one another. Bench labor within the cell and recreation taken individually in one's private little yard were the only diversions. There was to be a strict regimen of isolation and contemplation. All contact with the outside world was to be avoided. The reading of Scriptures would furnish the offender with the moral guidance necessary for reform.

A structure which would permit such a program required a unique and original design, and the building constructed was certainly innovative. To seal it off from society, physically as well as symbolically, the institution was surrounded by a stone wall, 30 feet high. Prisoners were kept in completely self-contained cells designed to eliminate the need or occasion for mingling with others. Thick cell walls prevented communication. Plumbing in the cells enabled the prisoners to remain in the cells indefinitely. This was the first public building in this country to use hot water heating and flush toilets.

In general, the building effectively accomplished what it was intended to accomplish—the removal of offenders from the community, their isolation from each other, and the provision of an atmosphere of solitude so that work habits could be learned and moral lessons contemplated. One of the earliest of the stream of European visitors to this famous institution wrote in 1835:

> *Solitary imprisonment is not only an exemplary punishment but a powerful agent in the reformation of morals. It inevitably tends to arrest the progress of corruption. In the silence of the cell contamination cannot be received or imported. . . . Day after day, with no companions but his thoughts, the convict is compelled to reflect and listen to the reproofs of his conscience. He is led to dwell upon past errors, and to cherish whatever better feeling he may at any time have imbibed.*

Charles Dickens came in 1842 and was appalled at the effects of solitary confinement on men and women and children. He wrote:

> *I believe it, in its effects, to be cruel and wrong. In its intention, I am well convinced that it is kind, humane, and meant for reformation; but I am persuaded that those who devised this system of prison discipline . . . do not know what it is that they are doing. I believe that very few men are capable of estimating the immense amount of torture and agony which this dreadful punishment . . . inflicts upon the sufferers. . . . I hold this slow and daily tampering with the mysteries of the brain, to be immeasurably worse than any torture of the body.*

With the opening of the Eastern State Penitentiary, a reform ideology was realized which would serve as a prototype for later American penology and much of the world's subsequent penal planning. Shortly after, in New York State, there emerged another philosophy of corrections which became a "rival" of the Pennsylvania System. The New York penal system adopted in the state penitentiary at Auburn a regimen of isolation of prisoners in cells in the evening but congregation in workshops during the day. This represented a stance antithetical to the code of penal administration recommended by the Pennsylvania Prison Society. Of special significance, however, was that the Auburn System represented only a variation on a model. The model itself, the use of imprisonment, was not questioned. This acceptance of the concept of penitentiaries represented the real triumph of the reform ideology, and penal institutions sprang up all over America and then throughout the world.

The hulking institutions which arose throughout the

country bear all too vivid witness to the acceptance of this new type of response. The endurance of these monolithic structures is surpassed only by the tenacity of the assumptions and attitudes on which they were founded: the cause of the crime is located in the individual offender; he should be punished for his acts; behavior is modifiable; and isolated institutions are appropriate settings in which to modify an individual's behavior. America had created a theory, reformation by confinement, and the system has been unwilling to abandon it although it has proved unworkable.

And today, after a century and a half of failure of penitentiaries, "lock them up" remains the basic response of society toward people convicted or even suspected of breaking the law. It has replaced the "flog them" or "off with their heads" of previous times. And lock them up we do.

If the prison has been a failure, the cause is not usually the wardens and other officials who run them. Many of these men and women, in fact most whom I have known in my long career, are good people. They often came into corrections with an optimism and a zeal for making their institutions more responsive to the needs of the people. If some of them became pragmatists—even pessimists—it was because the system changed them more than they changed the system.

There are many reasons for this, but a fundamental one is that society itself has been, and still is, befuddled about crime. It has no consensus as to the presumed causes of crime, nor to its correction. Various causes have been attributed to the committing of crime over the years, and they have changed as comprehension of behavior and definitions of crime have changed. We found it useful then to examine the changing views as to the causes and correction of criminal behavior.

The earliest attempt to understand crime found the solution in the supernatural. When people's behavior was extraordinary, good or bad, it was attributed to the presence of supernatural forces. Humans were possessed by gods or devils. This concept became refined as theology developed and criminals became regarded as free moral agents who chose not to cooperate with divine laws. The shift is important because once a person was held to be voluntarily choosing a life of crime, his responsibility was used to justify the punishment placed upon him. Much of society's reaction toward criminals has been premised on the assumption that the lawbreaker acted exclusively on his own. The possibility of his being influenced by the social, psychological or biological forces in his world was not considered. Crime then was a perversity to be punished and the response was primarily retribution.

With the ascendency of science and the accompanying belief that the world and its working could be logically understood, the role of the divine diminished. Man's position in the world order changed. He was no longer seen as a helpless pawn. He now investigated and studied the laws which governed the behavior of his kind, and he expected to use his knowledge to shape and maintain society. Many leading thinkers addressed themselves to understanding criminal behavior. Different scientists and philosophers pursued different intellectual avenues, and a variety of explanations of behavior emerged. Criminal behavior was variously attributed to biological, psychological, or social forces, and society created correctional responses in accordance with these theories.

For most of modern history, students of criminal behavior chose to focus on man in isolation as the key to understanding the cause of crime. As long as man alone was studied, it was inevitable that causation and the corresponding correctional response was centered on him. Man should be exiled; man should be executed; man should be mutilated; man should be imprisoned; man should be treated; man should be educated; man should be reformed.

The social sciences, however, brought different outlooks. Crime was seen as the inevitable outgrowth of the society's system of allocating goods and services, or the result of individual developmental patterns and family structures, or the product of faulty training or education. The role of the many disciplines in analyzing crime can be elaborated, but their collective point is this—if crime is to be successfully confronted by society, its causes must be known, and those causes go beyond the individual. People live in social settings and are subject to physical and psychological forces. To deny or to disregard the influence of these forces on man's behavior is unrealistic. Correctional responses to criminal behavior must therefore be directed not only at the offender, but also at the malfunctioning of his environment.

Though the social scientists have had increasing influence in the development of correctional responses to crime, their influence has been far from absolute. In fact, many persons of influence have opted to ignore causation in determining correctional treatment. Sentencing, they hold, should be on a purely legal basis not influenced by psychiatric and sociological theories of causation. The speculations as to cause by behavioral scientists have led to the establishment of programs aimed at treatment, the effectiveness of which has not yet been demonstrated. In some quarters it is believed that grave injustices have been inflicted on prisoners by placing their fate in the hands of behavioral scientists whose questionable evaluations determine the course and often the duration of a man's "correction." The more moderate critics of the efficacy of behavioral science would, however, be willing to continue to support professional investigation of the causes of crime, and to make available to convicted offenders on a voluntary basis a host of services and programs predicated on those assumed causes.

The understanding of criminal behavior and responses to it, as we have seen, have varied throughout history. The vast majority of responses have been focused on the criminal, with little or no attention paid to the responsibility for that behavior which could be imputed to the situation in which the criminal behavior occurred or from which it grew.

The purposes of a society's correctional system are influenced by two main factors. Initially, it depends on what a society includes in the definition of corrections, and where it places corrections' boundaries. For example, if a society defines corrections as the caging of lawbreakers in bleak institutions, this will certainly place limits on the goals which corrections can realistically be expected to achieve. By contrast, a community with unrepressive attitudes might include the provision of basic health, education, employment, and welfare services to its offenders as part of its corrections. The goals and the setting of this kind of corrections would then be different. The second main factor determining correctional goals is the moral-ethical orientation of the community, and the relative emphasis it places on individual rights as opposed to collective security.

The Purpose of Corrections

Over the centuries the most fundamental purpose for penal institutions has been *punishment*. Through them society takes its toll for crime. Punishment by legitimate authority has been held to be an improvement over the private settling of feuds. Moreover, it has been argued that the administration of punishment to known lawbreakers preserves the integrity of the rest of society providing the public reaffirmation of values. Those with a moral view also assume that punishment has cleansing, expiating effects.

Corrections has also been upheld as a *threat* and *deterrent* to potential lawbreakers. The belief that fear of an unpleasant penal experience would deter people from crime has been and is a main justification for the construction and perpetuation of hundreds of formidable institutions.

Both these goals — punishment and deterrence — are based on the assumption that criminal activity is the product of planned rational thinking, with full awareness of the consequences of an act. Some crime is; some is not. Irrational crime apparently cannot be deterred. For it confinement serves only vengeance and/or quarantine.

Penology, since the days when exile and transportation of criminals were the vogue, has recognized *quarantine* as one of its legitimate functions. The removal of criminals from the community has afforded the public a feeling of safety. It has been accepted as a valid purpose of correctional institutions, even by those persons who reject the morality of punishment or doubt the effectiveness of deterrence. Recently, however, thoughtful students of correctional institutions are concluding that the supposed protection afforded by the quarantine function is more illusion than reality. They hold that the prison experience contributes to more serious, if delayed, criminal activity.

A fourth goal of corrections is *rehabilitation*. It is the goal which makes the greatest demands on the correctional system in terms both of facilities and programs. Rehabilitation assumes that criminal activity is in some way caused by a deficiency or abnormality in the criminal. The goal then is to bring or restore the offender to a state of adequacy in the deficient area. Such areas of assumed inadequacy have been moral, physical, mental, social, vocational, and academic. If the assumption is made that crime results from inadequate functioning in one of these areas and it is further assumed that the criminal can indeed be changed, then an appropriate correctional response is to fill the gap through preaching, education, physical or psychological therapy, counseling, or vocational training. Of all the correctional goals, rehabilitation is perhaps the most elusive. First of all, there is no commonly accepted definition of rehabilitation, and secondly it assumes that the person to be rehabilitated shares or should share the values and motivations of the keepers, teachers, and therapists. In other words, turning troublesome lawbreakers into respectable adherents of traditional values is at the heart of the goal of rehabilitation. An obvious question is now being raised, "But what about the increasing group of new prisoners who do not accept the traditional goals of American society, and who, in fact, consider themselves to be political hostages?" The number of those who end up in the correctional system and who do not want to be corrected or rehabilitated poses a serious threat to the champions of rehabilitation.

Another function of corrections is said to be *integration* of the offender with his community. This is the most recently formulated purpose of corrections and it is certainly the one least observed. Correctional literature abounds with references to the desirability of using the community itself as the principal instrument of corrections. The goal of integration is based on the assumption that it is the poor "fit" of the offender and the community that is the cause of crime. Unlike the other objectives, this one requires that the system look beyond the individual in isolation and work at production of a better interaction between people and the world in which they live. A correctional program with this aim would be essentially different from those designed to meet the other goals. Utilizing the "fit" concept, a program aimed at integration does not remove men from their society. Rather, the community itself becomes the correctional response. Whenever possible, men stay in their normal social situations where they are supervised and assisted by correctional personnel. Both the community and the offender become targets for change.

The correctional administrator suffers from our failure to understand the causes of crime and our ambivalence about how to correct it. There are also other forces, some outside his control, that determine what he can and cannot do.

There is, for example, enormous fragmentation and that

fragmentation is a major cause of deficiencies in corrections today. This system — many observers prefer to call it a nonsystem — is operated by all four levels of government: federal, state, county, and local. There are federal prisons, state prisons, county prisons, and local jails. There are federal, state, and county probation services, parole services, police services, and court services. Some correctional programs are operated by the executive, others by the judicial branch of federal, state, and local government. No one plans for the whole system. Indeed, there is very little planning even for the parts of the system. The squeaky wheel gets the oil. This results in the adoption of policies which are not programmable, and programs whose basic conflicts preclude implementation.

There are also economic limitations. The generally unsatisfactory condition of our correctional process reflects the lowly status of the people caught in it. Should the number of middle and upper class persons convicted for drug offenses, opposition to the Vietnam War, and politically inspired crimes continue to escalate, either the laws will be made more tolerant or the correctional services will be upgraded. But as long as the majority of offenders are poor, uneducated, and of minority groups, the correctional slice of the public budget will remain small, and the overall response will be repressive. Imprisonment has proved the most expensive and least effective of the various correctional responses. The irony of it all is that there will be insufficient funds for more productive alternatives so long as the bulk of correction's resources goes for prisons and jails.

Moreover, there is incompatibility of goals and programs. Various goals of corrections produce conflicting programs. The rehabilitative goal, for instance, brought psychiatric services, individual counseling, and a host of self-improvement activities. These, for the most part, were superimposed onto basically punitive, repressive regimens and settings. The result is such incongruities as a therapeutic session in a counselor's office immediately followed by confinement in a dehumanizing cell, or a work release program in which an offender works all day in the community at his normal job, and then returns at night to be stripped naked and body-searched, to eat dinner without a knife, and to be locked in a cage. The effect this split program has on the man is destructive and results from society's vacillation between its desire for punishment and its commitment to assist the offenders toward becoming functioning members of society.

And there is still another factor in the correctional process over which the administrator has little, often no, control. It is intake. Who will come to prison? The warden can be reasonably sure of one thing. Most of his clients will be poor and members of one or another of the current outgroups. There have always been individuals in society who constituted a criminal outgroup. At different periods to be poor, indolent, insane, sick, intemperate, jobless, or dependent could insure membership in the "outgroup." The embracing of certain religious or political ideologies could also cause inclusion in the outgroup and subsequent repression.

If we look at the characteristics of these outgroups in America over a span of time we can see that certain qualities have been dominant. They were usually poor, troubled, dispossessed, foreign-born, and uneducated. There is currently one major change, however. Immigrants no longer monopolize society's correctional attention. Today the predominant outgroup is native born, but black. Some social theorists suggest that it is necessary that a society have an outgroup. In "correcting" that group, the society's values are reaffirmed and its fiber strengthened. That may or may not be true. What is important is that the legal process which precedes the correctional one has historically been used to maintain the economic interests and moral standards of selected people, while disposing of those who challenge those interests and standards. Legislators, police, and courts—not the warden—control that process.

The State of the Art

Pretrial Detention

In the United States today there are over 4,000 facilities, mostly county and local, which detain persons on behalf of the criminal justice system. They are usually called jails. On an average day they collectively hold a population equivalent to that of Hartford, Connecticut—160,000. In the course of a year they will confine up to 4,000,000 Americans. Only 15 of our 50 states can claim so large a population.

These jails have two prime functions: (1) to hold accused or convicted persons who are between arrest and disposition within the criminal justice process; and (2) to provide confinement, frequently now termed "correction," for minor offenders serving short sentences usually less than a year in length.

A majority, the percentage growing each year, fall within the former category—those being held for trial or other disposition. They are usually referred to as "the untried" though many have actually been tried and are awaiting appeals or other dispositions.

The people are a diverse lot. They include both men and women, young and old. They are traffic violators, misdemeanants, and felons. Drunks are the largest single category of admissions, but drug abusers and mentally sick people also plague the jailers.

On an ordinary day a typical detention facility will have among its population first offenders, situational offenders, professional criminals, and violent men and women prone to act out their personality disorders. It will house parole violators en route back to prison, soldiers and sailors awaiting return to military jurisdiction, and recently convicted felons awaiting transfer to the state or federal penitentiary.

It will also hold nonoffenders—material witnesses; accused persons, complaints against whom will be dropped; and tragically, many individuals who are totally innocent. Some will be held but a few hours while others will wait months, as long as 18 months, for their day in court.

In short, the typical jail is a catchall for society's unsolved problems including the sick, the weak, the inadequate, the occasional offender, the chronic thief, the vicious, and the innocent. But above all, it is a depository for the poor and the friendless. The very poor, though many, wield little political influence. Perhaps this explains why our jails are so miserably conceived and designed.

The jail as a detention center has a unique function—to insure an accused person's appearance for trial. Except for capital crimes, bail bond and release on recognizance may also be used to insure appearance no matter how serious the alleged offense. A bail bond is simply a money guarantee that may be secured if an alleged offender has either money or a good credit rating. In order to be released on personal recognizance—that is, without bail or confinement—the alleged offender is investigated and must have a sufficiently high stability rating.

The poor do not have money for cash bail. They do not have sufficient credit for bail bond. They often do not score high enough on the stability scale to gain release on recognizance. They consequently fill our jails.

Bail is not infallible in insuring the accused's appearance for trial. In some jurisdictions 5% to 10% jump bail. Release on recognizance properly run has a better record, but it also fails to produce a significant number of persons at court. This is part of the price a free society pays for treating as human beings persons who are and should be presumed to be innocent and treated accordingly.

The planners and operators of most of America's jails appear to make no such presumptions, take no such risks, and show no such concern for human values. Their overriding preoccupation is to hold. The be-all and end-all of their operations is security. And this they achieve effectively, but crudely. They do produce at court almost all those whom they are required to produce.

This almost absolute emphasis on security was evident in the plans and operations at the 26 jails and adult detention centers which we visited during our study. A few words about these is in order. They are located in the East, Midsouth, Deep South, Midwest, and West Coast. Some are operated by cities. The largest is in New York while the smallest is in a municipality of less than 10,000 inhabitants. The South has many such towns with surprisingly large jails. Twelve were county facilities — small, medium, large, and very large. Four of the jails we visited are operated by state governments. One houses only women, two are for men only. The rest receive both sexes. Juveniles are accepted in half of the facilities we visited. All but two hold both untried and sentenced prisoners. One accepts only the untried, while another receives only those serving sentences. Three receive pre-release inmates from the state penitentiary.

One had not yet been occupied on the day of our visit. Four had been opened within the year preceding our inspection. Fifteen were built between 1959 and 1970. The other four were older but were of significant architectural or programmatic interest to warrant inclusion in our study.

In planning the facilities which we saw, the administrators, consultants, and architects involved apparently developed their design programs around the following assumptions:

(1) Jailers are not wise enough to recognize which inmates might try to escape. They, therefore, must apply maximum custody provisions to all.

(2) Jails must be designed to compensate for the inadequacies and transience of personnel.

(3) Jails receive the most destructive elements of society, who have, during confinement, much idle time for the venting of

their destructive impulses. The masonry, hardware, and furnishings, therefore, must be virtually destruction-proof.

(4) Jails must be built as cheaply as possible. Since the concrete and hardware needed to provide the desired level of physical security are expensive, costs must be kept down by housing detainees in wards and by keeping the amount of activity space provided to a minimum.

Unfortunately all of these assumptions are quite correct. Every experienced jailer knows that considerable numbers of his inmates—even a large majority of them—are not going to attempt to break out. These can be confined under relaxed and inexpensive custodial conditions. But he knows, too, that the most inoffensive of prisoners, for reasons unknown to him, do occasionally attempt to escape. Because the prediction of inmate behavior is so uncertain, he quite understandably builds with tool-resistant steel and reinforced concrete for all.

And so it is with manpower. Often jail personnel are the flotsam and jetsam of the patronage system. The job specifications as well as the pay are low. The winds of political fortune shift and so do patronage job holders. This is especially true of sheriffs who in many jurisdictions cannot succeed themselves. The result is a less than professional group of jail managers and guards who usually are not able to differentiate between the very secure and the insecure sections of their jails.

Moreover, county and city governments which usually run the jails are the most poverty-stricken of all echelons of government. They seldom provide their jail wardens with anywhere nearly enough staff required for either good custody or a modicum of treatment. It is, therefore, understandable that jail planners compensate for human shortcomings with dependable alternatives like sally ports, closed circuit television, and interminable layers of iron grilles.

We agree with sheriffs that jail inmates are often destructive. However, we are convinced that the planners of the jails which were visited, jails representative of the most recently constructed detention facilities, shortchanged humanity when they opted so overwhelmingly for security. These planners have played fast and loose with fundamental constitutional safeguards. Also in making trade-offs to insure unequivocally the appearance of the accused prisoner in court, the builders of jails have contributed to the development of criminal attitudes and behavior in those being held. These trade-offs are largely manifested in the dehumanized environment—most normal referents are lacking—and in depersonalizing the treatment.

As investigators we undoubtedly hold certain convictions that affected our responses to what we saw. These are some of the attitudes which we took with us into the jails we visited:

(1) Government's highest purpose is to enhance the poten-

tial for a higher level of humanity of its citizens. Jails are run by governments and should share that high purpose.

(2) The untried are presumed innocent until found guilty in court. Most untried remain in the community while awaiting trial. They prepare their defense, work, enjoy the companionship of their friends and relatives, recreate, and even procreate. The untried who is confined is presumed to be just as innocent as his fellow man who is out on bail. There is no justification, therefore, for his exposure to degrading experiences, nor his subjection to a plethora of denials beyond those inherent in confinement itself.

(3) The untried should be given all the assistance necessary to prepare his defense.

(4) The untried should be assisted in maintaining his community ties and fulfilling his responsibilities to those in the community, particularly his family.

That means that the pretrial detainee should not be subjected to indignities or denied community contacts. He should not endure mail censorship, no-contact visiting, or excessive limitation of his physical movements. He should be permitted recreation, afforded privacy, allowed newspapers, magazines, law books, and his own clothes. He should have access to medical and other needed treatment. He should be protected against moral contamination and physical abuse. Since he has not been convicted he should not be punished and hence should not be held in circumstances equivalent to those for convicted persons. The present contrary practice seems clearly to violate existing constitutional guarantees.

Moreover, we are sure that imaginative jail administrators and creative architects can design detention facilities that subscribe to our convictions about the dignity of man and the presumed innocence of the untried. We do not think it would be easy, but nevertheless it is possible and very, very desirable. It is certainly not being done now.

Here are some of the things we saw which led us to so severe a condemnation of recent jail construction.

Our first impression of almost all the new jails we inspected was that they were designed in hypocrisy. Often built as part of a criminal justice complex or civic center they are frequently, on the exterior, inoffensive and even attractive structures. The approaches are attractively landscaped, sometimes even including fountains and reflection pools. One warden proudly noted that no bars are visible to outsiders — a now frequent ploy.

The overwhelming impression, once inside, is that the modern American jail, like its predecessor of the last century is a cage and has changed only superficially. The concepts of repression and human degradation are remarkably intact.

Our initiation to jails was a visit to a reasonably new regional facility in an Eastern state. The guard, sitting in

*Serene and
aesthetically pleasing
exteriors
often belie
rigid security
and oppressive
interiors.*

his bulletproof glass control room, pushed the button that opened the outer of a series of electrically operated grille doors. "Grille" means "bar" in the lexicon of the prison industry. We entered. On the right was a door leading to a reception area for new admissions. Across that door was stenciled STRIP AND FRISK.

We were later to find that every jail we visited had a similar room and a similar procedure. Here an individual—even in the crevices of his body—is searched in the name of security. We thought that there must be a better way. Later, we learned that similar strip and frisk procedures were standard at release as well as admission. We could not conceive that such an exit search would offer much in the line of security. We were told "it's in the guidelines" and was to prevent the "kiting" of unauthorized letters. This was our first face-to-face encounter with a procedure which, in our judgment, exceeded the requirements of preadjudicated confinement itself. There were to be many more.

The intake area is more than a place where one merely loses clothes. It is at this point that a person loses contact with one's spouse, family, employer, friends, personal belongings, money, community, and all other symbols of individuality and humanity. The stripping is symbolic of the new naked and exposed status. The newly admitted inmate, innocent or guilty, is now a nonperson. He is allowed one telephone call before the doors are shut behind him. He is now an item which must be processed. Dignity and pride are significantly eroded, perhaps irrevocably.

A captain in a shiny and expensive new West Coast jail said it all. In describing the delousing procedure in which a paint spray gun was used he joked, "We say that the man who runs this particular job here is getting on-the-job training for spraying cars, and he can get a job doing that after he is released."

An individual who has been committed to a detention facility spends only a short, if traumatic, time in the admission section. Not so the housing area. There he may spend weeks and months. We talked to some "untried" who had been in confinement over a year and a half. The housing environment therefore is the primary contributor to the detention experience.

It is important to see jail housing in perspective, and so a simple comparison with state correctional institutions may help.

In the majority of new state correctional institutions the importance of the housing area is diminished by the availability of other activity space. The convicted felon spends the majority of his days in the shop, the school, the gym, the athletic fields, the auditorium, the dining room, even the chapel. The detentioner, however, spends almost all his time on the cellblock, which is—for practical purposes—his only real world during confinement.

room for sentenced offender

multiple occupancy cells

an inside cell

blocked outside view

There is a second important difference. In the correctional institution all the inhabitants are serving sentences. They have been found to be guilty. A little of the Spartan might be expected in the cellblocks, their furnishings and their surroundings. The detention facility on the other hand holds persons presumed to be innocent. It could be anticipated, therefore, that the housing environment there might approach the normal. Not so. It is not that way. In fact, it is just the opposite. The planners of many new state and federal correctional facilities for convicted felons, which we visited, have moved toward normalcy. They have begun to provide rooms rather than cells. Privacy is beginning to be respected. Often the dayrooms are comfortable. The colors are restful. Rooms look out on landscaped gardens.

But the housing areas of most of our jails, even the new ones, are still essentially animal cages. Call them any other name — cells, squad rooms, dormitories — they are still cages.

Jail planners and the steel fabricating companies which supply the hardware have identified, as far as we saw, four kinds of sleeping quarters: rooms, individual cells, multiple occupancy cells, and open wards or dormitories.

Rooms have solid doors and provide privacy; they also have security-type windows and, quite possibly, views. Privacy negates easy surveillance; a window, even a barred one, can be breached; and a view of the outside world, as one sheriff put it, "makes the poor coot homesick." Wherever an exterior view might be possible the windows have exterior solid screens to block the view. We saw rooms in only one of the 26 detention centers which we visited.

Cells, single or multiple occupancy, were the most prevalent type of housing observed. Cells differ from rooms in that they have grille fronts. Privacy is surrendered on behalf of easier surveillance. These open grilles are the first elements of the cage syndrome. Other elements will be discussed later. From a security point of view, cells can be outside, semi-outside, or inside. The outside cell has as one of its walls the exterior wall of the building. Moreover it can have an outside window with all that that means in terms of natural light, ventilation, and possible vistas. It, however, is only escape-proof if a sufficiently vigilant staff is available. In our jails that is not the usual condition. Therefore outside cells are hardly ever recommended. We found them present in only three of the 26 adult detention facilities visited.

A semi-outside cell has the grille front, like an outside cell. However, the living space does not extend all the way to the exterior wall but is separated from it by a security corridor. This type of housing unit may have a barred windowlike opening enabling the inmates to view the outside. It, therefore, has some of the advantages of the outside cell while offering less opportunity for escape.

Inside cells are the most secure and subsequently the most popular with jailers. They are also the most cagelike. Usually they are built in back-to-back rows separated only by a utility corridor. They have grille fronts. Additional grilles separate the cells from the exterior walls and windows.

All these types of cells—inside, outside, and semi-outside—may have either single or multiple occupancy. The standards of both the American Correctional Association and the National Jail Association recommend single occupancy cells. Many states have also stated in their guidelines for jail construction a strong preference for the single cell. Only a few state legislatures, however, have translated these preferences into law. Single occupancy cells are preferred for the following reasons: (1) The single cell provides maximum security from the escape point of view; (2) it provides most flexibility in classification and separation of prisoners; (3) it provides maximum protection to jail personnel by not requiring them to deal with more than one unruly prisoner at a time; (4) it helps prevent homosexual activity; (5) it assists in the elimination of fights, physical exploitation and other forms of difficult behavior; (6) it limits the degree of contamination between more and less sophisticated inmates; and (7) it provides privacy.

Even though single occupancy cells—next to the single room—offer the untried more of the protection and privacy his status of presumed innocence requires, they are more expensive in terms of both money and space. They are therefore usually eliminated during the preliminary stage of jail planning. In their place are substituted two-, four-, six-, and eight-man cells or open wards.

The open wards are probably the most costly in terms of human values—sexual exploitation, moral contamination, physical exploitation, lack of privacy, and danger to staff. Moreover they do not permit classification or separation of prisoners. Guards and inmates with whom we talked all over the country referred to open wards as "jungles." Both jailed and jailer despise them. But in monetary terms they are cheapest to build and therefore are built.

The open wards which we observed ranged in occupancy from 12 to 60. They were usually crowded. Both single and double-deck beds were used. Toilets were invariably unscreened, open to view by all, and in close proximity to adjacent rows of beds. Space saving was the open ward's virtue, we were told. Many jailers with whom we talked regarded the jail's function as merely the warehousing of men. Dormitories are the most inexpensive warehouses.

In those states which do not, by law, require single occupancy, multiple occupancy cells have become a far from perfect compromise between the very expensive single cell and the least expensive but very unsatisfactory open ward. Multiple occupancy cells provide for more control, more diversified assignment of inmates than open wards, and they are less expensive than single cells to build because less steel, locking devices, and plumbing are required. All the major objections to open wards, which we have already expressed—lack of privacy, moral contamination, subjection to homosexuality and other exploitation are also, in degree, faults of multiple occupancy cells.

The housing units of a few jails which we visited were constructed on multiple levels known as tiers or landings. The cells on upper tiers were reached by iron staircases and long balconies into which the cells opened. This type housing appears to be going out of style for at least five reasons: (1) surveillance is made more difficult; (2) the cellblocks became unduly large; (3) heating and ventilating problems are created; (4) the noise level is especially high; and (5) occasionally, and mysteriously, people fall off the higher level balconies.

We discussed noise with several guards, inmates, and former prisoners. They told us that the noise level in all housing areas of jails is intolerably high. Built of steel and masonry, void of rugs, curtains or other sound-absorbing materials, and plagued by innumerable automatically operated grille doors which incessantly clang when opened and closed, these cellblocks sound like boiler plate factories. Many inmates cited the high noise level, lack of privacy, and poor lighting as the three most disturbing problems in the jail environment. Lights in most dormitories and cellblocks remain on all night making sleep difficult. Yet lighting levels are often too low for comfortable reading even in the daytime.

Natural light was almost nonexistent in three of the largest and newest jails. Instead of responding to the need for quiet and natural light the architects and jail planners opted for security. We saw little evidence of regard for human considerations.

In many of the "modern" jails which we visited, so-called dayrooms were provided adjacent to or in the housing areas. We saw two general types. The first and most prevalent consists of a long narrow area running lengthwise along the

Cavernous interiors
produce problems
of noise, heat,
and light.

Neither privacy
nor relief
from boredom
is offered
by dayrooms.

face of the cells. The grille fronts of the cells form one wall while a parallel grille forms the second.

The other type of dayroom avoids the long corridor effect, but retains the custodial advantage of being immediately within the security area of the cellblock. In this arrangement, the cells occupy one end of the cellblock while the dayroom occupies the other end. This type, except for the walls of bars, is more likely to resemble a room.

Both types of dayrooms described are usually surrounded by partitions of masonry and/or tool-resistant metal and bars, and by a security corridor from which a guard can safely observe the activities. Entrance is via security vestibules consisting of two alternately opening electronically operated grille doors.

Toilets are provided in the dayrooms, so that the inmate does not have to return to his cell. For surveillance purposes the toilets are left unscreened; as one guard said, "To avoid hanky panky." Time and time again in our jails, an apparently reasonable objective like surveillance works insidiously and inexorably toward an unreasonable end—dehumanization.

above and below: dayrooms

enclosed rooftop recreation

These dayrooms are uninviting and uncomfortable. They are furnished either with benches or a unique invention, the prison table. This is a metal or Formica square connected to the floor by a heavy metal tube. Welded to the tube, like four spokes, are four lesser tubes at the ends of which are fastened four disklike stools. The chief advantage of the prison table is that it is virtually indestructible. Moreover, no one can use it either to clobber an officer or another inmate or to spread the grillwork in an escape attempt. It is also intolerably unpleasant to sit on for any length of time. Many prisoners, therefore, prefer the floor.

In several of the jails that we visited the bleak dayrooms were the only alternative to spending 24 hours per day in a cell. The choice, actually, was between a small cage with no television and a larger cage with television. Many, of course, chose the television. Jailers, and wardens of correctional institutions too, have found the television to be a most inexpensive placebo. Frequently the choice of television is no choice at all, because policy requires that the detainee spend the day in the dayroom. As one warden put it, "They'd wear out the mattresses if we let them stay in their cells."

Generally these dayrooms with their television, occasional ping-pong, and unending card games provide the only recreation available to the untried prisoner. In two of the larger facilities, rudimentary libraries were available with the books being brought to the cellblocks rather than the inmate going to the library. Three had fairly large outside recreational areas but two of those were rarely used because of insufficiency of staff. Two new large urban jails had recreation areas on the roofs, though one was not used, and the other allocated only one hour per week per inmate. Still another had a combination gymnasium-dining room. This seemed a strange arrangement to us because eating and exercising were the two most popular activities and one seemed always to be in conflict with the other.

We observed three different types of dining arrangements. (Correctional people and jailers don't call dining "dining." They call it "feeding" which suggests, it seems to us, a passive and inhuman quality as in feeding the stock, or feeding animals at the zoo.)

The larger jails which we saw had central dining rooms in which food was served from steam tables, cafeteria style. The newer ones all were equipped with the four-man prison-type table, previously described. Prisoners seem to prefer central dining primarily because it offers them an opportunity to escape the boredom of the cellblock and see old friends from other housing units. Moreover there is a better chance, apparently, of getting more and better food.

However, central dining is not popular with many of the jail administrators with whom we talked. Three things they dislike are movement of inmates, congregation of large groups, and intermingling of prisoners from different housing areas. Central dining requires all three. Jailer after jailer stated that central dining was trouble. Moreover, it also requires space. Cell and dayroom dining is the practice, therefore, in most jails. As a consequence the eating experience contributes only to the maintenance of life. It provides none of the other essentials of a person's well-being and morale.

Sheriffs and jail wardens are required to receive and hold persons who have special problems. These include drunks, drug abusers in various withdrawal stages, potential suicides, and psychotics. Jailers are not physicians and most often do not have physicians readily available. Consequently, medical and/or psychiatric remedies for the behavior of these problem inmates are not available. The resort therefore is to physical solutions such as drunk tanks and isolation cells.

Drunk tanks are usually unfurnished cubes of masonry, steel, and grilles. In one new detention facility, however, the walls and floors were completely covered with a rubber-like but highly indestructible material. This was much softer than cement or tool-resistant steel and its purpose, of course, was to protect the falling, thrashing inmate from injury. The floors were sloped toward a central drain to ease the task of mopping. In several of these tanks the only equipment present was one or more of the combination stainless steel toilet-sinks which were usually operated by a guard from a valve located outside the grille. Some tanks contained only French-type (floor) toilets.

drunk tank

Isolation cells are small rooms containing usually no furniture or at best masonry or steel beds and an unbreakable stainless steel toilet-sink or a floor toilet. All wires, lights, and fixtures are recessed. We saw isolation cells with one or two parallel doors. Where there are two, the inside one is of grille, while the outside one is of solid steel except for small openings for observation and the passage of food, water, and other bare essentials. Even these small openings are equipped with closing devices. They render the rooms more or less soundproof, and totally dark. We talked to several inhabitants of these cells who described them as brutal and inhuman. In more than one instance, we found a man babbling to himself.

isolation cell

The physical plant and equipment of a jail does more than simply provide for receiving, housing, feeding, and inmate activities within the center. The building and equipment in large part determine the relationships between inmates and staff. In very few jails do inmates and staff mingle in the same space. Usually, they are well separated by iron bars because it is easier to control the inmates by using physical barriers than by establishing good inmate-staff relations, particularly when the latter requires an adequate number of qualified staff.

In many jails we saw guards walking up and down security corridors viewing inmates as they passed the dayrooms, cells, and dormitories. In some jails the officer sat in his office and looked at the images televised from cameras focused down the corridors of the housing units. Here, the concern is perimeter security; if nothing was going on in the corridor, or elevator, all was considered well. Anything could be going on in the housing unit itself because the cameras did not provide surveillance of these areas. The safety of the individual inmate was not considered important in the design of the closed circuit television system. In fact inmate safety is diminished by replacing the physical walk-around with the television system.

In the jail which had the highest degree of separation between staff and inmates the guards worked from within a glazed corridor. From here they watched inmates who were locked behind two sets of bars. From here they operated electronic devices which control the movement throughout the center. The overall effect of the jail was that of a giant machine for processing people. Guards were required only for activities which still require some human discretion—jobs which would be very costly to automate.

The trend in jail design is toward more extensive use of electronic equipment and steel bars. More and more staff functions are becoming mechanical in nature and the distance between inmates and staff is increasing. The result of these developments is an environment which is totally dehumanizing. The inmates are literally held in the system—they are mere items.

There are some people who are aware of the impact of the cages now being built to hold 'innocent' pretrial detainees. They are seeking to design facilities which are much less dehumanizing and allow for face-to-face inmate-staff relations. One of the centers being designed, though it is secure, houses detainees in small groups and in individual cells where some privacy is afforded. Ample space is provided for inmate activities and these spaces are organized to allow for maximum use by inmates.

We repeat that our system of criminal justice presumes the innocence of the accused until he has been tried and convicted. It is our premise, therefore, that a detention center for the untried should provide for normalcy in every way possible within the reality of confinement. There have, in fact, been several state court decisions which hold that detainees may not be punished. Yet it is abundantly apparent that confinement in facilities designed and operated for convicted persons is punishment. We have many times pointed out that the planners and builders of jails throughout the nation have repeatedly ignored the normalcy requirement in their intense pursuit of security. The visiting areas of the jails that we visited are both monuments to security and gravestones to normalcy.

Much later in this book we shall describe visiting accommodations in new institutions for felons serving lengthy state and federal sentences. We will not describe them here other than to observe that provisions are now made for privacy of conversation, contact, picnicking, and even, in some jurisdictions, sexual relations. The detention centers which we observed permit none of these.

The visiting areas were all the "no contact" variety in which the visitor and inmate are separated by a wall containing apertures through which they can attempt a conversation. The visitor is shoulder-to-shoulder with other visitors and has absolutely no privacy. Some of the apertures are mesh screens, others are small metal disks planted in glass partitions about lip high (if you are not too small or too tall).

Growing more popular is a dual telephone device. The visitors stand or sit immediately opposite each other separated by a tempered glass window. The use of a telephone on either side enables conversation to occur while prohibiting the passage of contraband. This telephone arrangement offers two additional advantages, according to jailers with whom we talked. First, it permits monitoring of conversations. Secondly, the telephones can be turned off at the end of the time permitted for visits—usually 15 or 20 minutes—thus effectively terminating the contact.

The jail isolates the inmate from the community and those who are dependent on him. The visiting arrangements in the jail reflect the attitudes of law enforcement authorities towards the detainee. He is of little worth. He is treated as if guilty. He is provided with little or no opportunity for preparing his defense. Thus being held in jail greatly diminishes his chances of defending himself; insures that his family's problems are compounded; results in his losing his job; and attaches to him the "jailbird" stigma. Jails contribute nothing to the detainee's or society's well-being.

Everything that we have written thus far suggests that jails contain only male adults awaiting sentence. That is, of course, not the case. They also contain women, children, and sentenced prisoners. The National Jail Census reports that in the time of the census (March 1970) 1 of every 20 jail inhabitants in the United States was female, another 1 in 20 was a juvenile. Nearly 9 in 20 were serving sentences.

Women and children represent very special problems but our sample of jails made few, if any, special provisions for them other than restricting their participation in even the very elemental activities available to the adult male.

The female and juvenile sections generally replicate in miniature the male cellblocks. Usually they are located on separate floors or wings and out of sight and hearing of the adult male population. Entry is via portals not utilized by the general population. The housing units are of the same reinforced masonry, grilles, electric gates, and barren dayrooms as found in the male section. The space available for the woman or child is even more circumscribed because usually they do not participate in work, dining, or recreation outside the confines of their cellblocks. The shortage of female staff places heavy restrictions on visiting and other activities requiring movement of any kind. As a consequence, the women and children whom we observed spent most of their hours either sleeping, sitting, talking, or participating in table games or handwork, such as sewing.

Many, many detained juveniles are confined to jails built for adults. Others are held in facilities built exclusively for juveniles. These are called by a variety of names, such as juvenile halls, detention homes, and juvenile court centers. Many of them are merely jails for kids, but others represent a marked change from the adult model.

*In general,
newer juvenile
facilities
give high
priority to
human values.
They often provide
complete programs
and attractive
physical facilities.*

As far as we could ascertain there are approximately 300 juvenile detention facilities in the United States. They received during 1970 nearly 500,000 youngsters. During our survey we observed only five such centers, all built since 1967, but during the past few years we have visited scores of other juvenile detention centers. Moreover we have studied many reports and surveys of detention services.

The juvenile detention home is a product of the juvenile court movement which started at the turn of the century. The devastating effects of the adult criminal justice system, and especially the jail, upon the frequently unsophisticated youthful offender, demanded a more appropriate response to the treatment of juveniles. The objective of the juvenile court and the detention home, spelled out in many juvenile court acts throughout the nation, is to provide the youngster with the care and treatment that he should, but usually does not, receive in his own home. It is not surprising, therefore, that the new detention centers for juveniles which we visited were relatively more homelike than the jails. They were also more adequately staffed. Jails throughout the nation have a 5.6 to 1 ratio of inmates to staff. Juvenile detention centers have a much more favorable 4 to 3 ratio. Furthermore, the juvenile detention services frequently employ more highly educated staff often including treatment specialists such as teachers and counselors.

As we spoke to detention home superintendents we were impressed that they, in contrast to jail wardens, usually saw security to be but one—though important—part of their responsibility. None ignored security. In fact we were told time and time again that there are only three justifications for placing a child in confinement pending a court hearing. They are these: (1) the child in all likelihood would not show for court if he were not detained; (2) he represents an immediate threat to others; and (3) he represents an immediate threat to himself.

All three of those justifications for confinement contain important demands on the detention home and on its staff for security and surveillance. They also represent a basic departure from the safeguards provided for adults where bail is a right regardless of the threat which the accused represents. The juvenile can be, and is, detained for what he might do. This amounts to protective detention for youth, something that is not permitted for adults in most jurisdictions. This denial of certain rights to children is, in effect, part of a contractual trade-off between society and its child. In return for a surrender of certain rights which are afforded adults the child is supposedly guaranteed the care and protection equivalent to that which a loving parent would provide. This is called *parens patriae*. The government acts to protect the defenseless child.

The new juvenile detention homes which we saw reflect this different emphasis. They are not cages. They often attempt to provide constructive activities and facilities for those activities. They are more adequately staffed than are the jails we visited. In several they give much more attention to human values. For example, they provide rooms rather than cells. Privacy is more likely to be respected. Dining is almost invariably a group activity. Visiting is open. Recreation is available and more varied. Attempts at rudimentary forms of milieu treatment are apparent. Schooling usually required by law for children under 16 is available, if only in rudimentary form. Often activities are coeducational.

Unlike the jails which depend almost exclusively on hardware for security the newer juvenile detention centers which we visited place much greater emphasis on program and staff activity to prevent runaways. While jails usually utilize "inside" cells the youth detention facilities have "outside" rooms. The jails have a superabundancy of tool-resistant steel bars; the detention centers depend on less obtrusive detention mesh or unbreakable glass. Almost all activity in the jail is confined to the cellblock. The youth detention centers which we visited utilize the entire plant for activity purposes. A much higher type staff seems to be required for the more personal kind of correctional program.

It was our observation that there is a correlation between the size of the detention units and the quality of both the security and the rapport that we observed. Housing units, for example, varied in size from 12 to 24. In the smaller units we observed camaraderie and much less preoccupation with control. In that center having the largest units we found a climate more nearly approximating that of the jail with the accompanying rigidity and grimness. There we observed a more punishing attitude on the part of the staff and a corresponding guardedness, fear, and overt hostility from the detentioners. It was in this latter institution that we also observed the use of closed circuit television. Previously we had seen it only in adult prisons and jails. Closed circuit television is an insidious device substituting an all-seeing electronic eye for the flesh and blood human supervision. Some remote person, watching a bank of several monitors, observes and reports on the most insignificant as well as the most private behavior. It was our conclusion that its questionable contribution to improved surveillance was negated by the personal insecurity and hostility that it aroused. Detention is a period of maximum uncertainty for a child. Every effort should therefore be made to increase the opportunity for natural interaction between the child and staff. Closed circuit television diminishes interaction thus adding to the child's manifold uncertainties, and in spite of the improvements over jails which many juvenile centers offer, juvenile detention in the United States is shockingly uneven and very often inadequate, even destructive. The national survey conducted in 1965 for the President's Commission on Law Enforcement and the Administration of Justice revealed that 93% of all juvenile court

jurisdictions lacked any detention facilities for juveniles whatsoever. As many as 100,000 children are, therefore, annually confined in lockups and county jails pending their hearings before the juvenile courts. Very few of those counties which do operate juvenile detention homes approach even remotely the minimum standards for program and plant. *Parens patriae* has miserably failed to protect the troubled American child.

A vignette from a visit to the juvenile section of a county jail on the West Coast captures, it seems to us, the corrosive contaminating nature of the entire preadjudication confinement process.

In the barren grilled dayroom of the girls' ward we found two teenagers. One was very pretty and the other, a runaway, quite plain. The pretty girl was vivacious; the runaway withdrawn. They were sitting on a bench talking together when we entered. After a few moments of introductory comments we asked, "Locked up in here, what do you miss most?"

The pretty one, without hesitation, shot back, "Speed, man, Speed. It makes you feel so good, so alive, so high. I miss men, too. Their bodies. Sex. Speed and men. That's what I miss."

The plain girl said nothing. She sat and stared and possibly thought that Speed and men might be just the answers to her unhappiness.

Institutions for Adjudicated Offenders

Over the years the form of the prison has changed. Dr. Norman Johnston has described these changes in the historical monograph published as a companion piece to this book. It is sufficient here to describe briefly the basic forms that have persisted and give some attention to those which are evolving.

The Basic Form

Many of the early prisons were built like spokes of wheels. The housing units, shops, and activity spaces radiated out from a central hub in which was located the control center. All activity and movement could be observed from that center. Many famous penitentiaries—Eastern State, Trenton, Rahway, and Leavenworth were built in the radial design.

The Radial Design

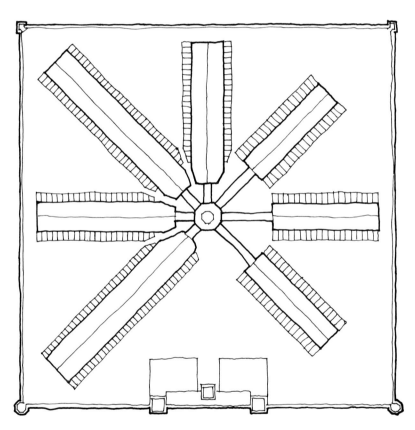

Eastern State Correctional Institution, Philadelphia, Pennsylvania

Camp Pendelton, U. S. M. C.

The only totally radially designed new institutions that we saw are the county jail in Charleston, South Carolina, and the Marine Disciplinary Barracks at Camp Pendleton, California. However, we did see many new facilities that utilized radial housing components in facilities that were essentially of other basic designs.

A second ancient prison form is based essentially on the layout of Sing Sing. Several maximum security prisons were built around the huge multitiered cellblocks, each of which contains up to 1,000 tiny cells that are characteristic of that New York penitentiary. Near the cellblocks and within the walled enclosure are separate buildings for administration, industry, eating, and other activities. Institutions of this type are still in use in many states. We have visited such institutions in Pennsylvania, South Carolina, Nevada, Colorado, Wisconsin, New York, Kentucky, West Virginia, Washington, and Illinois. Older prisons in several other states are built similarly. Because all these are old, and our concern is with contemporary design, we will not spend more time on them.

The Panopticon Prison

Jeremy Bentham spent a good part of his productive life trying to convince the British to build a prison designed in a circle with the cells located around the circumference and a guard stationed in the middle. One man could then maintain surveillance over an almost infinite number of prisoners. Britain rejected the concept but many other countries including Holland, Spain, and Cuba did build such prisons. The Cuban institution, opened in 1926, had a capacity of 5,000.

This kind of prison was a natural outgrowth of the utilitarian viewpoints of Bentham who had been impressed by the efficiency of an industrial revolution era factory. This factory, with its "all seeing eye" design, enabled production managers to view an entire manufacturing process from a single vantage point.

One circular prison was built in Pittsburgh in the 1820's but construction errors, especially regarding light, negated its usefulness. Surveillance was made difficult by the gloominess of the place.

One large *Panopticon* prison was built in the United States at Statesville, Illinois. Its dining room and cellblocks were built in the form of circles with control booths located in the centers. Even though Statesville is an important prison with the huge capacity of 4,600, it was not included in our itinerary because it is not new (opened 1919), and has not been copied elsewhere in the United States.

Although the *Panopticon* design never really caught on in America, its "all seeing eye" principle lives. Today in prison after prison, closed circuit television cameras relentlessly peer at inmates even in their most private moments.

Statesville, Illinois,
Panopticon *plan,*
exterior and
interior

The Telephone Pole Design

When prison programs actually changed and inmates began to move about frequently between school, shop, treatment, recreation, and housing areas, a new plan for prison architecture evolved which became known as the "telephone pole" design. The name describes the basic form. The pole is the long central corridor. The crossarms are the housing units, shops, schools, and support facilities. All movement is rigidly controlled by the design as prisoners can move from activity to activity by way of only one axis, and that is continuously supervised. With the resulting ease of surveillance it is not surprising, therefore, that almost all high security prisons which have been constructed in the United States in the last 40 years follow that design.

In our travels we visited Graterford, Pennsylvania, an older but classic telephone pole type prison. Opened in 1928 with a capacity of 2,000, it is surrounded by the second largest prison wall in the country. (Jackson, in Michigan, is slightly bigger.) From the entrance gate an enormously long central corridor stretches so far before one that the sides seem to converge at the far end. Five two-tier cellblocks, each containing 400 outside cells join the central corridor. Those housing units approach in length that of the main corridor.

Cellblocks of this length and capacity complicate classification, cause custodial problems, and foreclose the possibility of small group treatment efforts. The present warden at Graterford and his architects are struggling to design small units out of these mammoth cellblocks, but as of this writing they have been unsuccessful.

In addition to Graterford we visited several new maximum security institutions which utilize the telephone pole design. Two of these—the Federal Penitentiary at Marion, Illinois, and the Connecticut Correctional Institution at Somers were opened in 1963. Two others, Holman and Mt. Meigs in Alabama, were opened in 1969 and 1970 respectively. The reception center at Jackson, Georgia, opened in 1967, is also of the telephone pole design.

Two small, but secure, prisons which we visited also used this popular form. They were the Regional Correctional

Georgia Diagnostic and Classification Center, Jackson, Georgia

exterior view of cellblocks in telephone pole design

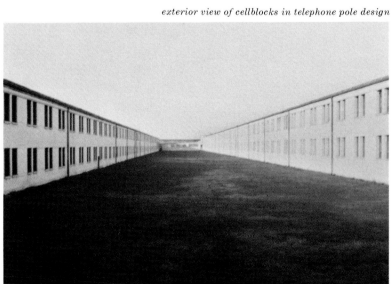

Endless corridors are typical of telephone pole designs.

Facility at Greensburg, Pennsylvania (opened 1966), and the Women's Institution at Canon City, Colorado (opened 1968). Another brand new correctional center for women, opened in 1971, is located on New York City's Rikers Island. It utilizes a modification of the telephone pole design that ignores one of the basic virtues of this prison form. The telephone pole ordinarily provides controlled and readily observed movement. At Rikers Island, however, the long corridor is serpentine, thus rendering total visibility from any one place impossible.

This popular design has one great virtue—security. All movements are via a central corridor. Shops, training facilities, and housing units are attached to the corridor thus making movements out of the building almost unnecessary. There are also very considerable disadvantages, especially to the human spirit of persons who are long exposed to such a choiceless, repetitive, controlling, and unstimulating environment.

A young architect working with our survey team, after his first visit to a telephone pole type prison, made the following observation, "There are two major problems there—overdetermination and the removal of referents."

To inhabit a setting (he called it a "context") is to be shaped by it. That setting normally provides the reference points necessary for exercising judgments, for acting, for growing.

In any setting, two conditions can destroy fulfillment of a human being. They are overdetermination and removal of referents.

Overdetermination, he said, is the condition in which everything—decisions, space, movement, and responsibility—is clearly or narrowly defined. All activities are scheduled. Social contacts are predetermined. The physical setting is limited and monotonous. The context is highly explicit, predictable, regimented, and offers little real choice. It is a condition in which groups can be easily supervised, where authority can be maintained, and one in which accountability for personal action lies beyond the individual.

The second phrase, removal of referents, means the inducing of uncertainty by cutting off ties with the past, by grossly reducing contact with people, places, activities, and ideas. It was accentuated in this prison by the denial even of a wristwatch. Daily and seasonal variations are lost. Thus uncertainty is induced, making it impossible for a person to predict, plan, decide, judge. The result, my young architect told me, is suspension — temporal, spatial, social, and psychological.

In time, both overdetermination and removal of referents result in constriction and atrophy. The person subjected to them stops growing, learning, feeling. In short, *confinement*, with its overdetermination and removal of referents, *prepares one only for confinement.*

This highly intellectual and philosophical response of a young architect seemed to describe precisely the nature of maximum security confinement in a telephone pole type institution where the long, barren corridors, the rows of identical cells, and the channeled movements all contribute to an experience that is anonymous and sterile.

The High-Rise We observed several high-rise jails in urban settings all over the country, but we saw only one high-rise correctional center. That was at Morganton, North Carolina, and it was opened on May 1, 1972, the day following our visit to it.

The high-rise jails, incidentally, are not different from all other pretrial detention centers visited except that they pile floor on floor of the cages we have described earlier in the book. The correctional center at Morganton is different. We could not, however, understand the reason for building a 16-story prison at the foothills of the Smoky Mountains on thousands of acres of open land.

The high-rise is, in effect, a modification of the telephone-pole type prison, but is built vertically rather than horizontally. It substitutes an elevator shaft for the long central corridor. All movement is via the elevator and can be minutely supervised. Control, almost absolute control, appears to be the hallmark of the high-rise correctional center that we saw. As many as 40 inmates eat, sleep, and participate in therapy and group activities on a self-contained floor. There is no way the inhabitants of one floor can associate with those of another without the approval of the administration. The top floors are devoted to segregation and reception and the floors below to housing. (This will be discussed later in other sections.) The lower floors contain the administrative section, industry, education, and treatment.

Because Morganton was not occupied except for a small cadre on the day of our visit, and because neither staff nor inmates could be interviewed about its strengths and weaknesses, we cannot speak to its effectiveness. The high-rise appears, however, to have most of the advantages of the traditional telephone pole prison and most of its disadvantages plus those special problems with mass movements that high-rise universities have experienced.

We saw ten new correctional centers each built around one or more courtyards with the enclosed buildings forming the external perimeters. At least seven of these were highly secure facilities yet their external appearances were largely void of the unattractive fences and guard towers usually surrounding the other secure correctional facilities that we visited.

The Courtyard Design

We found this type of prison design to be more appealing to us than most other forms for several reasons. Institutions so designed were attractive, often looking more like consolidated schools or modern suburban office buildings than prisons. Moreover, the very design, though secure, not only encouraged but actually required continuous inside to outside movement. At Yardville and Leesburg in New Jersey, Sierra Conservation Center in California, and Purdy in Washington, for example, one did not move from housing unit, to school, to work, to recreation, etc., along seemingly endless inside corridors. Rather the design demanded that people move in and out of the weather, be it warm or cold, clear or wet. Prisons are ordinarily places that dull the sensory perceptions. This design offers sensory stimulation. Several inmates commented that this lack of apparent crowding, the opportunity to get away from people, the ability to avoid constant physical contact caused less aggressive behavior. This is also characteristic of the campus design.

Sierra Conservation Center, Jamestown, California

New Jersey Youth Reception and Correction Center, Yardville, New Jersey

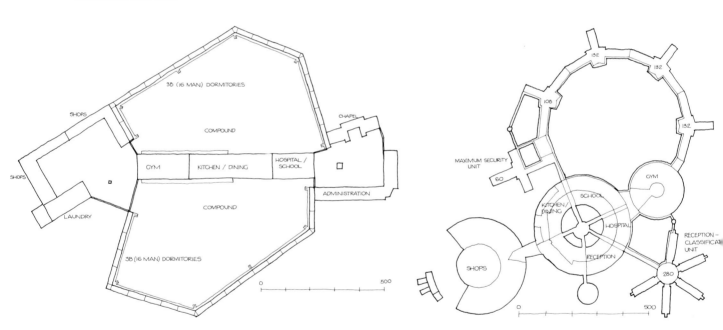

The Campus Design

A majority of the new juvenile institutions which we visited plus a growing number of correctional facilities for adults have been built in the campus design. Many of these are attractive, some exceedingly so. Open juvenile schools in Georgia, Wisconsin, Washington, and Texas have handsome buildings scattered over scores of magnificently landscaped acres. The Robert F. Kennedy Youth Center at Morgantown, West Virginia, an open federal facility for youth, is almost spectacular in its overall effect.

One of the most remarkable campus-type correctional centers for adults was opened in 1972 at Vienna in Illinois. Buildings looking much like garden apartments are built around a "town square" complete with churches, schools, shops, and library. Paths lead off to "neighborhoods" where comfortable "houses" provide private rooms in small clusters. Extensive provision has been made for both indoor and outdoor recreation. Academic, commercial, and vocational education facilities equal or surpass those of many technical high schools.

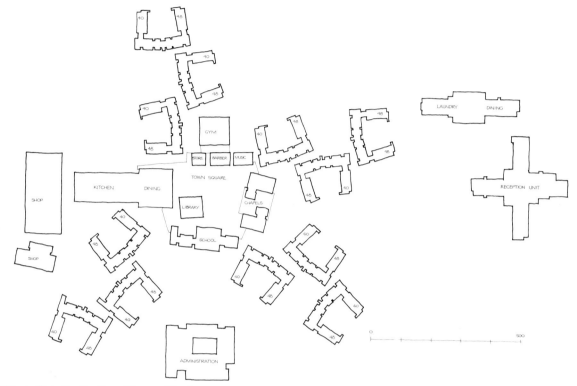

Illinois State Penitentiary, Vienna, Illinois

This correctional center has been designed for 800 adult felons. Unfortunately, most of them will come from the state's metropolitan areas many, many miles away. Today this open institution is enjoying the euphoria that often accompanies distinctive newness. One conjectures, however, about its future if and when urban prisoners begin to abscond into neighboring rural towns, and when developing community correctional programs siphon from the state's prison system many of the more stable and less dangerous offenders. Fortunately, and probably, this facility will not be rendered obsolete. The nonprisonlike design is flexible and will permit it to serve a variety of educational, mental health, and other human service functions.

The campus design is not limited in usefulness to open facilities. Some that we saw are quite secure. In California, Texas, and Pennsylvania, campus-type facilities surrounded by double fences serve escape-prone youthful offenders.

The planners of the exceptional correctional center at Fox Lake, Wisconsin, designed that facility so that widely spaced and attractive buildings are set on beautifully land-scaped acres. The winding walks and undulating contours break the monotony of flat Midwestern countryside. Yet a secure perimeter keeps escapes to a minimum. The Michigan Training Center at Ionia is similarly planned and exquisitely landscaped. The spaces are so vast that the deputy warden used a golf cart to transport us around its expansive acres. And it has even greater perimeter security than Fox Lake.

We even saw two campus-type prisons that had been built to serve maximum security functions—reception and classification. New admissions are the greatest custody risks for several reasons: (1) they are as yet largely unknown to the system; (2) many are undergoing severe adjustment problems; and (3) their correctional future has not yet been defined. For these and other reasons, reception centers that we visited—even those for children—were much more security conscious than other types of institutions.

On our survey through the South we visited three new reception centers in adjacent states. Two, opened in 1969 and 1970 respectively, were tightly built in the telephone pole design. These were geared to the fullest possible supervision, control, and surveillance of the inmates. Design and program choices optimized security. Buildings and policies restricted the inmate's movement and minimized his control over his environment. Other considerations, such as individual or social needs of the inmate, were responded to only as they conformed to security requirements. Trustworthiness on the part of the inmate was not anticipated; the opposite was assumed. His compliance was not sought; it was not even necessary.

The third, opened in 1967, is of campus style with several widely separated buildings occupying 52 acres which are enclosed with a double cyclone fence with towers. Movement is continuous as inmates circulate between the classification building, gymnasium, dining room, clinic, canteen, craft shops, handsome outdoor visiting area, and dormitories.

Men who are not specifically occupied by the demands of the classification process are encouraged to involve themselves in a variety of recreational and self-betterment activities conducted all over the 52-acre campus. An open air visiting patio with picnic tables and multicolored umbrellas supplements the indoor visiting facility which is used ordinarily only in inclement weather. The relationship between staff and inmates appears casual. Movement is not regimented. Morale appears high and escapes are rare.

We were in general favorably impressed with campus-type facilities. They are much more attractive; they are not congested; and they cause inmates and staff to move in and out continuously, thus providing sensory stimulation so often missing in closed facilities. Moreover, they allow or require inmates to make choices, thus reducing the overdetermination that is characteristic of prisons. At the same time, if designed properly, they provide the security required by properly assigned populations. And most important one does not become hypnotized by the effects of the endless corridors, the clanging locks.

BASIC DESIGN FORMS OF 60 NEW CORRECTIONAL CENTERS

TYPE	MAXIMUM SECURITY	MEDIUM SECURITY	OPEN	TOTAL
RADIAL	1	0	0	1
PANOPTICON	0	0	0	0
TELEPHONE POLE	10	8	0	18
HIGH-RISE	0	1	0	1
COURTYARD	4	5	1	10
CAMPUS	2	11	17	30
TOTAL	17	25	18	60

Location of Correctional Facilities

Perhaps the most significant change in the recently defined objectives of corrections can be summarized by the word "reintegration." Both the President's Commission on Law Enforcement and the Administration of Justice (1967) and the report of the Task Force on Corrections of the National Commission on Criminal Justice Standards and Goals (1973) consider the successful reintegration of the offender into the community to be the primary goal of corrections today. Other writers and opinion leaders also place this first on the agenda for the improvement of corrections. This new goal represents a complete about-face.

Historically the correctional institution was based on the concept of separation, punishment, and isolation. Prisons, both rural and urban, were built to keep the prisoner in and the community out. It simply was not considered necessary to make provisions for visiting, family relations, community involvement, or work release; and there was no effort to secure staffs that were professional and of a racial balance to match the racial makeup of the inmates. The old corrections succeeded in isolation and control functions but was markedly unsuccessful in preparing offenders for life in the real world.

Reform leaders in the field reasoned that isolation was in itself a basic cause of the failure of corrections. They planned new methods with which the offender would be treated, as far as public safety would permit, in the community. For those few who required imprisonment, the confinement experience should permit maintenance, even strengthening, of family and community ties; it should involve all the educational, vocational, health, research, and social services of the larger community; and it should be staffed by persons harmonious in life style and ethnic background to that of the offender. Our survey team, therefore, hoped to find most new correctional facilities in or near major population centers and universities in order to maximize the opportunity for interaction between the offender and the creative and corrective forces that exist there, as well as to be near to the largest source of the inmate population.

This hope and the reality that we found were two different things. With the exceptions of jails which were usually located in the county seats and small special purpose facilities such as halfway houses, all of the new correctional institutions which we visited were rurally located. They were far removed from universities, unable to be reached by pub-

Newer facilities are often located in rural settings, while cities have grown around older facilities.

lic transportation, and seemingly designed to discourage citizen and community involvement. In addition they were usually staffed by rural persons unsympathetic, even antipathetic, to the aspirations, life styles, and ethnic values of the prisoners who were mostly black, brown, red, and urban.

Some facts relative to the location of major new correctional facilities for adult males which we visited are reported in the following table:

LOCATIONS OF 23 NEW CORRECTIONAL INSTITUTIONS FOR MEN

	INSTITUTION	ROAD MILES TO STATE'S LARGEST CITY	POPULATION OF SUPPORTING COMMUNITY	PERCENT MINORITY INMATES	PERCENT MINORITY STAFF
EAST	MAX SECURITY	125	3,000	55	1
	MAX SECURITY	35	6,000	42	9
	MAX/MED SECURITY	70	2,500	49	11
	MAX/MED SECURITY	40	4,000	50	20
	MED SECURITY	140	2,500	54	4
	MED SECURITY	100	35,000	65	1
	MED SECURITY	30	3,200	2	0
SOUTH	MAX SECURITY	450	1,300	51	2
	MAX SECURITY	240	8,000	54	0
	MAX SECURITY	65	2,500	55	11
	MED SECURITY	110	9,000	unknown	unknown
	MIN SECURITY	100	2,500	50	20
MIDWEST	MED SECURITY	275	44,000	unknown	unknown
	MED SECURITY	236	6,000	52	25
	MED SECURITY	157	13,000	45	7
	MED SECURITY	90	2,500	24	6
	MIN SECURITY	455	2,500	40	5
WEST	MAX/MED SECURITY	172	6,500	unknown	unknown
	MED SECURITY	435	15,000	20	1
	MED SECURITY	425	2,000	52	5
	MED SECURITY	120	9,000	31	2
	MED/MIN SECURITY	33	20,000	59	14
	MIN SECURITY	60	27,000	49	17
	AVERAGE	172	9,900	45	8

In view of the current emphasis on community corrections, we investigated the reasons behind the selection of predominantly rural sites for new institutions. In the discussions with scores of correctional officials in many states, a variety of reasons was advanced. There were six main reasons: (1) powerful legislators demand that institutions be built in their rural districts especially if unemployment there has become chronic; (2) citizen lobbies fight the establishment of correctional facilities in urban neighborhoods; (3) many states already own large tracts of land in the more isolated areas or land is cheaper in the country; (4) correctional administrators think they can get more desirable (code for white) staff in rural America; (5) some officials have an honest Jeffersonian belief in the curative virtues of a bucolic setting; and (6) historical accident.

An interesting anecdote about an historical accident was told to us by the warden of a Rocky Mountain prison. During the transitional days between territory and statehood, a committee of legislators was touring, apparently assigned the task of locating a site for the new state's capital. They were a hard-drinking lot, and in a brawl tore up the hotel in which they were staying. In the resulting settlement the state acquired the hotel and surrounding land. The state's first penitentiary was built on those grounds in 1861. It is still in use. Recently two new institutions, one a medium security facility for men and the other a women's prison, have also been built there. Correctional practices in that state in the late 20th century were thus preordained by a drunken brawl a century earlier.

Many new institutions which we visited were built on land adjacent either to older prisons or other state facilities. Examples include Leesburg, Yardville, and Skillman in New Jersey; the city complexes on Rikers Island in New York; Holmesburg in Philadelphia; Mt. Meigs and Holman in Alabama; the women's prisons and the medium security prisons in both Colorado and Nevada; the Women's Correctional Center in Oregon; Somers in Connecticut; a complex at Hagerstown, Maryland; Morganton in North Carolina; and a variety of facilities in California and Texas. The major advantage of placing a new institution adjacent to an already existing one is that the public does not howl. Most often citizens use every pressure conceivable to block the construction of a correctional facility near their homes.

On the other hand, powerful rural legislators on key committees have frequently demanded as the price of their support that a proposed new facility be built in their districts if unemployment there is chronic. This is certainly a worthy reason, but we never once heard it advanced as a reason for selecting an urban site though there is severe black unemployment in the cities. Community correction, reintegration, and corrections' need for the auxiliary resources of the cities and universities all have been sacrificed to the pressures of pork barrel politics. The results are sometimes outrageous. In one large state an enormously expensive new prison was recently opened hundreds of miles from the state's great metropolitan center from which a large proportion of its inmates come. In another state the influence of one powerful legislator dictated that a huge complex of institutions be built in his town of less than 5,000 people which was located 200, 110, 100, 150, and 500 miles away from the state's five largest cities. The director of this vast complex has developed an interesting rationalization to justify his remote, self-contained institutions now that the national thrust appears toward community-based corrections. His philosophy has its roots in the earliest precepts of both the penitentiary and reformatory systems. He holds that the primary source of delinquent behavior is in the offender's environment and the secondary cause is his inadequacy to cope with that environment. The response is to provide institutions in the most remote areas where the offender is protected from those environmental influences and, at the same time, exposed to a wholesome life style predicated on traditional rural middle class values. Compensatory education, claimed to be better than that available in the community, would then supposedly equip the inmate with the tools necessary to face his own world again some day.

This model of corrections clings to the traditional idea that remote congregate facilities are the solution to delinquent behavior. Yet similar institutions built to serve other residual elements of the population—the poor, the indolent, the mentally ill, the retarded—have never experienced notable success. They have, one by one, been replaced by programs in the community.

Exponents of community corrections similarly assume that the offender's problems are related to the environment, but hold that he must learn to deal with those problems where they are—in the community. Institutions, if required at all, should be in or close to the city since that is where most inmates originate. They should not duplicate anything—school, recreation, work, entertainment, or clinical service—that is available in the community. The offender's entire experience should be one of testing himself in the very setting where he will one day live. The treatment process, they hold, demands that each offender constantly examine with his peers the quality of his adjustment. This second model, that of community corrections, is still largely untested, but its advocates think it promises to move corrections toward more venturesome and hopeful days.

Location and Race

The preference for white rural staff over "the bottom of the barrel" available to corrections in the more competitive urban labor market was obviously a pervasive reason why administrators accepted, even sought, rural sites for their institutions. One correctional official after another with whom we talked gave lip service to the current rhetoric about community corrections; they freely admitted that professional staff was most difficult to recruit in rural America; and they complained about travel problems for prisoners' families and friends; yet they nevertheless have repeatedly opted for the rural setting with its ample pool of steady, white guards. This practice might have been relatively unimportant when America was still predominantly a farm country and life styles—rural and urban— had not yet hardened in their contrasting molds. Then prisons were viewed almost exclusively as places of quarantine. Where better than the "boon docks"? But those are no longer valid reasons nor have they been for a quarter of a century. America has become increasingly urban. Life styles and values, born not only of population diversity but of ethnic differences, create understanding gaps wider than the miles which separate city dwellers from farmers. The rhetoric, if not the purpose, of corrections has also changed. The ultimate objective now being expressed by reformers is no longer quarantine but reintegration—the adjustment of the offender in and to the real world. Many prison officials, needless to say, do not accept this notion.

The continuance of prison construction in the sparsely populated sections brings with it serious disadvantages: (1) it is impossible to utilize the academic and social services or the medical and psychiatric resources that are concentrated in the cities; (2) professional staff—teachers, psychologists, sociologists, social workers, researchers, nurses, dentists, and physicians—have been hard to recruit; (3) contact with friends, lawyers, and relatives of inmates, important to the reintegration process, is made more difficult; (4) meaningful work and educational release programs are practically impossible; and (5) most importantly, corrections has become a divided house dominated by rural white guards and administrators unable to understand or communicate with the inmates who are often black, Chicano, Puerto Rican, or from other urban minorities.

The location of institutions in rural America has had, it seemed to us, especially pervasive effects on the federal prison system. Senior officials in federal institutions which we visited outlined the trade-offs between rural and urban sites in the same terms as those already described. Their views as expressed to us were these: "In the rural areas you get the very best type of white, mid-American line staff; but it is admittedly more difficult to recruit blacks and professional staff which are available in the cities." They would settle for competent white guards every time. Because over the years this kind of reasoning has been prevalent in the Federal Bureau of Prisons, the whole system is dominated on every level—guards, lieutenants, captains, deputies, wardens, and central office staff—by rural white Americans. A major Midwestern federal prison had, for example, at the time of our visit, five black staff persons in a complement that exceeded 200. Thirty percent of its inmates were black.

To avoid a federal Attica,* the Federal Bureau of Prisons is now feverishly attempting to recruit black staff, but its task is complicated by the remoteness of its facilities.

The problem of black recruitment is sometimes less severe for states than for the federal government because the distances between each state's prisons and its cities are not so vast as in the federal prison system. The table on page 48 points out that the state prisons which we visited nevertheless had disproportionately low minority representation on their correctional staffs. Of all inmates in 20 correctional institutions for male adults which we visited 45% were from the principal minority groups. Only 8% of the staff were black, brown, or Spanish.

The placement of institutions in rural America is not always, however, the product of crass politics, economics, racism, or philosophic rationalizations. In one very large state, for example, we met an affluent rancher who had moved heaven and earth to convince the state's administration and legislature to build a correctional complex in his exceedingly rural county. We asked him why and his answer was simply, "I want to hold my grandchildren on my knee." Confused, we asked for clarification. The young men, it seems, do not stay down on the ranch. They go to the university and then to the cities. If only there was interesting and challenging work in the county they might come home after college, marry, and raise children. Corrections is, he reckoned, interesting work.

Two types of institutions seemed to us to present very special site selection problems. The first is the correctional facility for women. For whatever reasons, the treatment of women by the criminal justice system has, until now, been different from that given men. Perhaps fewer commit crimes, certainly fewer (1 to 6) are arrested. Still fewer are indicted and convicted, and, in comparison to men, very, very few (1 to 30) are confined in state correctional institutions. North Dakota, for example, confines 1, Wyoming 2, Montana 8, Utah 14, West Virginia 28, Nebraska 44, Minnesota 55, and even populous Pennsylvania confines only 127 women.

Location of Women's Institutions

The consequence of this, unimportant in the old days of isolation penology, is that most states have only one facility for women, inevitably far removed from the homes and communities of a large proportion of the confined women. Some states have no facilities for women. Their female offenders are boarded in adjacent states. The Rocky Mountain state of Wyoming is an example. It boards its few female prisoners in

*Attica, we all know, is the rural New York State Penitentiary where 32 prisoners and 11 hostages died during a rebellion on September 13, 1971. One of the underlying causes of that riot was the alleged indifference of white guards to the hopes, aspirations, and humanity of black and Puerto Rican inmates who comprised 80% of the prison's population. On the staff there was only one Spanish American and no black.

Nebraska's Reformatory for Women. Eight states have no special correctional facility for females, but confine their women offenders in separate wings of the penitentiaries for men.

The federal system provides perhaps the most horrendous example for remoteness. It is true that nearly 200 of the Federal Bureau's female prisoners are confined in the co-educational correctional institution on Terminal Island near Los Angeles, and a few others are boarded out to several state facilities. The overwhelming majority of federal women prisoners, however, are confined in the Federal Reformatory for Women at Alderson, West Virginia. That part of southern West Virginia is breathtakingly beautiful, but extraordinarily isolated and extremely difficult to reach by highway, air, or train. The town of Alderson, incidentally, has a population of less than 2,000, and the nearest city of any consequence is Charleston, four or five difficult travel-hours away. It hardly represents an ideal location for practicing the new penology.

Some of the new facilities for women, including three that we visited, are located on land occupied by men's prisons. Several arguments were presented to support this practice: (1) the land was available; (2) professional staff such as physicians, dentists, chaplains, and nurses could serve both facilities; (3) central services including heat, sewerage, purchasing, warehousing, and business administration need not be duplicated; and (4) male custodial staff from the larger prisons could assist the matrons in times of trouble.

Though these arguments might appear persuasive, our impression was that there was at least one good reason for locating the women's facility distant and administratively separate from the men's prison. Essentially it is that the satellite women's institutions which we visited are much more controlling, custody-oriented, and repressive than are those which were independent of the influence of male correctional philosophy and practice. The satellites use the terms (warden, maximum security, count-up, lockup), the hardware (television surveillance, segregation cells, barbed-wire topped fences, electrically operated exterior doors), the controls (supervised movements, frequent head counts, body searches, and closely supervised correspondence and visits), and have the same preoccupation with escapes and homosexuality as do their adjoining male counterparts. In fact, one satellite women's prison which we visited was, in our opinion, the most controlling and repressive institution that we saw, and its lady warden seemed determined to surpass her male associates in their own methods.

Location of Reception Centers

A second type of institution that presents very special site selection problems is the reception and classification center. This is a relatively new invention born of the proliferation of correctional facilities in many of the states. North Carolina, for example, has 79 state institutions for adults and 9 for juveniles. California has a total of 21, New York 28, Florida 13, New Jersey 10, and Ohio 13, and these totals do not include small satellites such as road, forestry, farm and work camps that many jurisdictions operate. These states provide many institutional options and the courts are incapable of prescribing the proper place of commitment. Reception and classification centers have therefore evolved. They receive commitments directly from the courts, evaluate the new admission using a variety of diagnostic tools, and then determine the offender's proper placement in the total system.

All such centers operating today are not distinct and separate facilities. Quite the contrary. In most states, the reception and classification function is performed in a section of one of its institutions—usually the maximum security one. Most new prisoners therefore start their correctional experience in the most confining, most severe, and most repressing part of the state's system. After a period of observation, testing, and interviewing, an assignment supposedly reflecting the best marriage between the inmate's needs and the system's resources is made. Today 13 separate, usually new, reception centers for adult felons and several juvenile centers are in operation. We visited 6 of the newer ones.

The fundamental site considerations for institutions serving the reception and classification function are these: (1) proximity to sources of intake which are, of course, the many county court houses; (2) proximity to the facilities to which the classified prisoner will be transferred; and (3) proximity to professional staff as well as specialized diagnostic and research resources. Needless to say these three considerations may each suggest different spots on the map as ideal site choices. The first requirement might point to the state's center of population density; the second to a small isolated place where the state's prisons are concentrated; and the third to the state's major city or university.

We saw new reception and classification centers which met one or another of these three site requirements. Alabama's Mt. Meigs is located very close to the geographical center of the state, as is Georgia's Jackson. Neither is especially convenient to the majority of its state's other prisons nor to a major university. Colorado's reception center, on the other hand, is attached to the maximum security prison and within a half dozen miles of most of that state's correctional facilities. It is completely remote, however, from Colorado's major cities and universities. Florida's Lake Butler is a long state away from populous Dade County (Miami), Tampa, and Pensacola, but it is very close to the huge prison complex at Raiford and reasonably convenient to the University of Florida. There seems to be no place which meets all requirements.

Pennsylvania has, it seemed to us, a sensible solution. That state has been divided administratively by the governor into six common human service regions. There happens to be a major correctional facility in five of those six regions. A section of each has been designated as the reception and classification center for its region. Inasmuch as four of these prisons are located near or in major metropolitan areas (Philadelphia, Pittsburgh, Harrisburg, and Wilkes-Barre/Scranton) and the fifth is convenient to Pennsylvania State University, all of our three site requirements seem to have been met as well as possible.

Size   The penitentiary did not start big but became big. By the middle of the 19th century all the idealism and hope that went into the invention of the penitentiary was replaced by a pragmatism that held that confinement was a valid end in itself. Prisons could not correct or reform, but they could separate the offender from the rest of mankind. A kind of warehousing developed. Prisoners were stuffed into tiny cubicles stacked tier upon tier. Movement was tightly scheduled and regimented. Human needs were ignored. Economy of operations became the essential element of prison management. The bigger the prison, the more economical the operation. And prisons grew. Penitentiaries to house between 2,000 and 5,000 men were built in Texas, Oklahoma, Pennsylvania, Tennessee, New York, Virginia, Georgia, Florida, California, Illinois and Michigan (the biggest). Many small states such as Delaware, Hawaii, Maine, Montana, North Dakota, Rhode Island, South Dakota, and Wyoming built prisons no larger than 500 and as small as 250 to house their smaller inmate populations. In spite of these exceptions the average prison for men built prior to 1960 was constructed to hold 1,100 inmates. The extremes were 250 and 4,800.

The inevitable consequence is the development of operational monstrosities. It is impossible to remove large numbers of men from the free world, isolate them together in the unnaturalness of huge prisons, and not have management problems of staggering dimensions. The tensions and frustrations inherent in prisons of any size are magnified by the herding together of large numbers of troubled people. The result is the evolution of a prison goal that, when stripped of all the correctional rhetoric, is simply, "Keep the lid on." Regimentation, discipline, control—not treatment—have become the correctional preoccupations. Dehumanization is one of the major results.

The correctional officials with whom we talked recognize this clearly. To our inevitable question, "If you were just starting to build this place what would you do differently?" the first answer almost always was, "I'd make it smaller." This seemed to be true however big or small the institution.

A superintendent of a treatment center for girls said it this way:

If I were designing an institution from scratch, I would make it small. This place with 144 girls is too big. Before we expanded we operated out of one building with only 38 girls. That was some institution. What I learned then was that the quality of an institution depends almost completely on the quality of the relationships between the staff and the girls. When an institution gets big you deal with girls through echelons of commands. In that kind of place it is harder to maintain an atmosphere that says, "I care."

The warden of a correctional center for men was equally emphatic:

The first thing wrong with this place is its size. We have 1,026 people here and that's too big for any institution. Take a look at this place. Anyone with an ounce of honesty about him would admit that it was designed for warehousing, not corrections.

And it was.

Some effort has been made in the last few years toward building smaller institutions. The average size of new major institutions for adults included on our itinerary is 770, far below the 1,100 average of the pre-1960 period. The average capacity of juvenile institutions that we visited is 215.

In several states, notably Michigan, Texas, and California, attempts have been made to maximize the supposed economic advantages of bigness while maintaining smaller operational units. In each of these states large juvenile complexes were visited that consisted of relatively small, and often autonomous, units located adjacent to one another and served by central facilities such as water, treatment, sewerage, power, warehouses, and medical services. In spite of these attempts at fragmentation, they still had the flavor, including the regimentation, of very big facilities.

Any attempt for us to state dogmatically a preferred size is a meaningless exercise unless size is directly related to the operation of the center. But it seems to us that the following should be determining factors in deciding the size of a correctional facility:

(1) The size of a correctional center should not exceed the inmate population from the immediately surrounding region with perimeters not more than one hour travel distance. Centers should be located near urban areas where staff, program support, and program opportunities are available.

(2) The size of a center should be small enough to enable the superintendent who is responsible for operations, programs, and center regulations to know the name of, and to relate personally to, every inmate in his/her charge. Unless the inmate has contact with the person who has policy responsibility, and who can assist the inmate with his personal difficulties and requests, the inmate will recognize that he is

in a center, the prime purpose of which is to serve the system and not the inmate. The reverse is also true. If the superintendent does not have contact with the inmates, his decisions will be determined by the demands of the system and not the needs of the inmate.

(3) The size of a center should be such as to enable the effective and efficient operation of its programs. In other words, the size of a center should be a function of what it is trying to do. A center providing a large amount of individual counseling and therapy for high risk inmates, for example, should be of a size to make efficient use of its professional staff and to maintain the level of supervision necessary without regimentation, surveillance equipment, or repressive hardware.

Because of the problems inherent in land acquisition, a correctional complex exceeding the above size requirements can exist if it is made up of several separate small centers with different functions and different programs.

Security—Perimeter

While preparing for this study we wrote to the heads of the correctional agencies of the 50 states asking that they classify for us each of their institutions according to degree of security. The director of one of the country's largest systems, a former president of the American Correctional Association, replied succinctly:

> *We operate one unit without armed correctional officers and security devices. At all other units we take a dim view of any attempts to escape.*

With the exception of juvenile institutions, which are generally, but not always, less custody conscious, the above statement accurately describes the prevailing attitude of most correctional officials in the United States. Security is the *sine qua non* of the American correctional system today, as it has been since the invention of the penitentiary nearly two centuries ago. It is our observation that corrections utilizes five principal methods to prevent escapes:

(1) Employment of personnel who are taught to be vigilant. (2) Classification of prisoners. Inmates are assigned to institutions according to their likelihood to escape. For example, those considered most likely to escape are assigned to very secure institutions. (3) Threat of severe punishment to those who do escape. (4) Building of facilities to provide for a maximum of internal surveillance and control. (5) Provision of sufficient perimeter security for each institution to cope with the apparent custody requirements of the inmates who are assigned to it.

Because people are so unpredictable, a person who is not an escape risk at one moment may become one overnight. Corrections, therefore, practices overkill. It is the opinion of most wardens to whom we talked that no more than 10% to

20% of all prisoners require maximum custody, yet 56% of all adult prisoners in the United States are in structures built to serve the maximum security function. These institutions depend heavily on very secure perimeters.

The older prisons are usually surrounded by high, thick masonry walls with gun towers built like turrets. The entrances are forbidding and the overall appearance grim. We did not see many new prisons that utilized masonry walls though we met many wardens who yearned for them. The economics of prison construction has, however, rendered these walls obsolete.

The nature of perimeter security of the new prison is partially captured by the following excerpt from our field report describing our arrival at a new maximum security institution in the Midwest:

> *As our team approached we became vividly aware that security was central to the operations there. A sign on the perimeter of the 1,000 acres directed us to an intercom device. We were directed by a disembodied voice to state our names and purpose. Having complied, we were ordered to wait while a check was made with the central control center. Finally we were directed by the voice to a parking space. As we surveyed the double wire fence we noted that the guards in two of the towers were following our progress through binoculars, rifles at their sides. We felt anxious, uneasy, and very unwelcome.*

Incidentally, at this secure institution we immediately saw a vivid example of the basic conflict in corrections—that between custody and treatment. The unfriendly voice from an unseen person, the guards with their binoculars and rifles, the strands of barbed wire, all seemed to say, STAY OUT. Immediately inside the front door, on the green felt bulletin board, were the words, "Welcome, W.G. Nagel and Associates from The American Foundation Institute of Corrections."

Such is the schizophrenia with which prisons are bedeviled.

*Modern towers
employ
sophisticated
surveillance
techniques.*

There are two basic elements to the perimeter security of every new maximum security and most medium security prisons that we visited. They are:

(1) A buffer zone. These new prisons are all rural and built in the midst of many acres of relatively undeveloped land. The land itself provides a buffer between the institution and the outside world. Usually signs proclaim the penal nature of the reservation and warn "unauthorized persons" to keep out. An ordinary, but interested citizen, or an inmate's relative, might well wonder whether he or she were "authorized" or "unauthorized." This buffer zone also provides lines of vision permitting guards to observe persons approaching or, when the event occurs, prisoners leaving.

(2) The fence. The new complexes of maximum and medium security prison buildings are almost invariably surrounded by heavy-gauge cyclone fences. They are usually double with open space between them. Frequently this open space is covered with white sand so that the human being will be silhouetted. Thus the person who is intent on escape must, after having climbed the inner fence, spend a fearful few seconds trapped between the two fences where he is in the sightlines of the marksmen armed with high-powered rifles and shotguns.

These fences are made even more secure by one or more of several special security features. These include aprons or concertinas of barbed wire around the fence tops and sensitive electronic sensory devices that sound alarms either when a person tries to mount the wire or is in no man's land between the fences. One women's institution which we did not visit has recently utilized laser beams. We also saw strategically placed gun towers manned by riflemen. Still other security features are pedestrian and vehicular sally ports. These are usually double and parallel with electrically operated doors which cannot be simultaneously opened. Thus a person on foot or in a vehicle entering or leaving the institution spends a few moments trapped between two gates while proving his identity and his right to enter or leave. There, too, he may be physically or electronically searched for possible contraband. Powerful floodlights insure that the darkest nights are as bright as midday. Closed circuit television cameras monitor doors, gates, and blind spots in the perimeter; and dogs sometimes roam between the dual fences.

If people have to be confined, it is usually against their wills and adequate perimeter security is vital. The results of alternatives that we saw were often, in our opinion, more ugly than the unsightly fences. For example, the opennness of new, unfenced institutions invites escapes that the administration then tries to prevent by rigid internal discipline, precipitous transfers to more secure prisons, or indictments for escape which result in long consecutive sentences. These constrictions and threats, it seemed to us, are even more devastating than are the barbed wire fences,

The roof,
protruding inward,
at Leesburg
New Jersey,
was designed
as a deterrent to
prison breach.

the television monitors, and the threatening riflemen. At least the latter are tangible and not hypocritical. The prisoner can make his peace with them. He cannot, however, accept the everchanging rules, the "chicken shit" supervision, the possibility of punitive reprisals, or fictitious concern so often insincerely expressed by correctional people in these terms, "We can't treat you if we don't have you."

The worst examples of perimeter security that we saw were architectural afterthoughts—not built into the original plans of institutions. Many of these facilities were built originally as low custody facilities. Frequent escapes eventually resulted in community protests and legislative dissatisfaction. The correctional officials responded with Rube Goldberg solutions. Around one institution composed of buildings scattered over an undulating campus of over 100 acres, a makeshift fence was constructed. It is so rambling that it is impossible to maintain or survey. It provides no impediment whatsoever to the escape plans of the agile inmates. It probably does serve a public relations purpose.

Around a tight little facility for youthful offenders, we found coil upon coil of barbed wire successively added as the inmates became ever more determined to abscond. In others we found ineffective locking devices which consumed valuable staff time for operating, monitoring, and repairing. In many we found barbed wire draped over and around gates, buildings, and yards. In still another, cowbells were strung on chicken wire to alert the armed guards to escape attempts. All of these, it seemed to us, were abortions esthetically, morally, and custodially. And they had negative effects on the operation of the institution. For example, we mentioned to a lady warden, whose prison was surrounded with improvised concertinas of barbed wire, that the women inmates likened the fence to that of a concentration camp. Her reply was "What do you think this is?" Innocently one of us suggested that it was a correctional center. She dismissed that with one word, "Blah." Her prison was precisely what the fence and the warden had defined it to be. She has since been replaced. Hopefully a different attitude came with her replacement.

Exclusive of jails, community correctional centers, and older facilities, our study team visited 60 new major correctional institutions. The following table summarizes the basic characteristics of their perimeters.

PERIMETER SECURITY

TYPE	MALE ADULT	FEMALE ADULT	JUVENILE	TOTAL
DOUBLE FENCE WITH TOWERS	19	0	3	22
DOUBLE FENCE WITHOUT TOWERS	0	0	2	2
SINGLE FENCE WITH BARBED WIRE	1	3	2	6
BUILDING FORMS SECURITY	4	1	2	7
BUILDING SUPPLEMENTED BY FENCE	3	1	0	4
OPEN	6	0	12	18
WALLED	1	0	0	1
TOTAL	34	5	21	60

It is our conclusion that architects have abdicated either to the hardware salesmen or to the dreamers in designing the custodial features of recently constructed correctional facilities. We found either an overemphasis on grim means of escape prevention or we found the open, fenceless institutions that constitute a perpetual temptation to the inmate to try to escape. We add only that the perimeter security is also often inadequately designed causing ineffective and unattractive improvisations, or the stereotyped barbed wire and towers that we have already described. It is our view that architects can and should do better.

Living Quarters   The term "total institution," currently in vogue among sociologists, very accurately conveys what seems to us to be the essence of the correctional institution. Control of mobility, repression of individuality, and an almost complete absence of participation in decision-making is generally the lot of the confined offender. Virtually every aspect of his daily existence is determined for him by others. If there is one pervasive characteristic of our current penology, it is that the inhabitants of correctional settings are *involuntary participants* in both a physical and social structure. This fact — the coercion and control inherent in correctional settings — is of highest importance in understanding correctional housing. A few other facts must be pointed out also.

Despite the departmental statements to the contrary, the housing probably is the item having the greatest impact on the total incarceration experience. Programs of various types may be attempted, actually implemented, or totally ignored, but *all* institutions must house those committed to them. This they must do even if nothing else is undertaken.

It is safe to assume that some institutions offer little more than housing from commitment to release. For many offenders then, the housing into which we put them is the "correctional" experience. Even those institutions which do operate therapeutic, educational, or recreational programs do not program for a man's entire day. When not being interviewed, educated, employed, or entertained, the large majority of incarcerated men are in housing units.

This stands in sharp contrast to living patterns or life styles in other institutions and certainly in free society. Prisoners spend an inordinate amount of time confined in their quarters. If for no other reason, this constant use of quarters makes it imperative that correctional administrators understand what the impact of correctional housing is on the incarcerated offender. Free people view their rooms in limited functional terms — a place to sleep, usually for eight hours a day. When a room's use becomes expanded to include recreation, eating, washing, and even more personal functions, the significance of that room is extremely heightened for its occupant. We must not, therefore, judge correctional housing by the same standards we would use with other housing. Rather, we must go beyond a routine description of the physical configurations we observed.

There is no part of corrections that offers so many contrasts, or more rationalizations to justify those contrasts, than housing. This is because many philosophies, purposes, and forces converge at that precise spot where the prisoner spends so much of his time — the living unit. There his basic social and correctional experiences are defined.

The two great penitentiaries that sired American corrections — Eastern State and Auburn — had different housing genes. Eastern, as we have already noted, was committed to separate confinement for 24 hours of each day. Its cells, therefore, were the beginning and the end of the prison experience and, accordingly, were built large. Each had its own outdoor recreation area. Even in 1829, these cells had inside plumbing and hot water heat. At Auburn, in contrast, the primary prison experience was labor in congregate factories. The cell was but a place to sleep. The prison planners therefore saw no need for big cells, with the consequence that at Auburn they were made very small—just tiny cages.

In the battle for penal supremacy, Auburn, at least in the United States, was the victor. During the next 100 years, one state after another built row on row of cages stacked tier on tier atop each other. Most of them were smaller than 50 square feet (the precise size of the closet of the room in which this is being written). Each contained a bed. Later, as prison populations grew, a second bed was added. A stool and a small table and a bucket for toilet purposes completed the furnishings. Later, the bucket was replaced by the prison water closet—a combination toilet, sink, and drinking fountain. Almost invariably, these cells had no windows. Open grille fronts permitted light, air, noise, and constant surveillance while denying socialization, movement, and privacy.

These awful, old cellblocks are still very much in use in most states, and this is tragic. But what is more tragic is that the housing units in many very new prisons are direct descendants of those monstrosities and very, very much like the original. They are, however, made worse by modern mechanical and electronic devices that still further reduce the human considerations. In true modern fashion and to prove that we are a concerned, humane, and feeling people, we now sometimes give our inmates pastel colored bars. Welcome to the 1970's.

typical multi-tiered cellblock

stark isolation cell

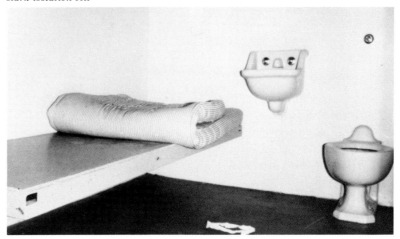

inside cell devoid of windows yet lacking privacy

One prison was built for 500 of the most intractable prisoners of a certain state. Because it has no gymnasium, no classrooms, miserably small dayrooms, and practically no industry, each man spends most of his prison life in a $5\frac{1}{2} \times 8$ foot cell with another prisoner. Each man has less living space than that provided by the surface of a typical bedroom door. There, because of the lack of program and recreational activity, the prisoners vegetate. Privacy does not exist. The cell toilet, for example, is pushed tight against the bottom bunk. As there is only one chair in the cell, the toilet stool serves as a second chair. It was the warden's observation that even a man and his wife require moments of privacy from each other. Here, he said sadly, privacy and human dignity are relentlessly sacrificed. We can think of few more gross forms of humiliation.

Tiny and crowded as the cells are, they are infinitely preferred by the prisoners to the congested dormitories where single beds have been replaced with double-decker bunks, where noise and night lights impede sleep, where privacy is nonexistent, where one can never be alone, and where television, beds, recreation, toilets, and showers are all crowded into the limited space. These crowded wards are, according to staff and prisoners, frightening jungles where predators assault their fellow prisoners for their possessions or their bodies.

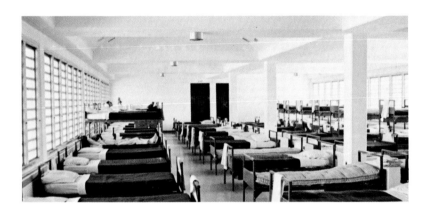

Among the reasons why the dormitories are such dangerous jungles is that officers are not physically present in them. At the end of each series of dormitories or cellblocks, there is a bulletproof cage where a guard sits, able to observe but not to control the living units. He is also inaccessible for relationships with the inmates. Men have been replaced by closed circuit television cameras which continuously scan toilets, beds, and corridors. Officers in the control center survey 20 or more television screens constantly. Both warden and captain thought these screens, which had poor pictures and unreliable performance, were almost useless, but they are fundamental to this institution's security. Bugging devices are also installed throughout the housing units, and sounds and voices are constantly monitored. These two items of modern electronics—the closed circuit television and the eavesdropping devices—have proven of marginal value as instruments of control, and because they replace men they have intensified the hateful, impersonal nature of some prisons. "Big brother" dominates the penal scene.

One inmate described the ever-present television camera in this way:

> *This is the only place in the world where a man can urinate, defecate, and masturbate knowing full well that some bastard is watching him on the boob tube.*

An inevitable consequence of this poorly designed, poorly staffed, and practically programless prison is the frightful deterioration of its inmates. Our psychologist observed that the emotional state of the men there was similar to that described by many observers of Nazi concentration camps. Responses were dulled and there was a great denial of feeling. Apathy and depression were everywhere. A college-educated inmate described four ways to pull time there:

> *(1) You shoot dope.*
> *(2) Find yourself a boy and make out sexually.*
> *(3) Burn yourself out reading.*
> *(4) Just sleep.*

The planners of this prison apparently were very clear as to its purpose. Simply stated, that purpose was to warehouse human beings as securely and cheaply as possible. Its housing units shouted this to us loudly and clearly.

Not all correctional housing that we saw is as depressing as that just described. We have already noted that corrections is full of contrasts caused by the differing functions of specialized institutions, their population differences (especially sex and age), fiscal considerations, and the conceptual—even philosophic—viewpoints of correctional administrators and architects. It is our conclusion, after viewing over 100 new institutions, that the last-named consideration is a more significant determinant of the nature of correctional housing than any of the preceding. Here is some of the evidence which led us to that conclusion:

(1) In a Western state, we visited a new prison for women. The basic belief behind its design is that women prisoners have to be watched every moment, that they should not be trusted. This prison was surrounded by barbed wire. The housing units were built in the form of a cross so that all corridors could be constantly overseen from one central control room. There were no dayrooms as such, but tables placed around the control room and under the eye of the matron served that function. There the women could play checkers or cards under constant and immediate supervision. Though the bedrooms were reasonably large and well glazed, there were no pictures on the walls, no curtains, and no colorful bedspreads. Everything looked very sanitary, dull, and unfeminine. The vista from the rooms included gun towers and concertinas of barbed wire. This plant and its operation reflected a point of view.

In Washington the new Purdy Treatment Center for Women serves an identical purpose and a nearly identical population, but it was conceived and built and is operated according to a completely different point of view. This difference is especially apparent in the living quarters.

Individual rooms are decorated to the tastes of the occupants. Colorful bedspreads and draperies personalize their quarters which are comfortably furnished. Each grouping of 16 rooms has a carpeted parlor complete with comfortable living room furniture, television, and a handsome fireplace. Adjoining the dayroom is a dinette for snacks, furnished with stove, refrigerator, and coffee percolator. The women hold keys to their rooms. The entire environment spoke the words *trust, individuality,* and *beauty,* and the views from the rooms echoed them.

The great contrast in the morale of those confined in these two institutions was very apparent. Each was designed to handle the entire female penal population of its respective state, yet this contrast alone suggested to us strongly that Purdy provided a positive public service while the other did not.

(2) At Vienna in Illinois in a single institution, one can vividly see the products of the philosophic differences of two sets of correctional officials and architects. In the early 1960's the state of Illinois decided to build a large minimum security complex in the southernmost part of the state. The original design provided for the construction of nine X-shaped structures of three floors each. One of these was built. Its housing units were large warehouse-type dormitories finished in gray cement block. The four legs of the X radiated out from a control center from which the officer could observe his hundreds of human charges. In that center there was a secure fortress from which, in case of disturbances, rifle fire could be brought to bear on the entire population without obstruction.

That was one conceptualization of a minimum security correctional institution. Before the eight other proposed units could be constructed, the correctional administration in Illinois changed. The original design was abandoned and a new architect employed.

The result was a vastly different institution. Its housing units, designed like modern townhouses, open onto what is called a "town square." This town square includes, as we have already noted, such facilities as the library, a barber shop, a commissary, game rooms, an educational building, chapels, and music rooms. There is a handsomely landscaped open mall or courtyard which has benches. It serves as a central congregating point.

townhouse-type housing

security with consideration for human values

The housing units themselves consist of several two-story buildings. Each of these has four wings of 24 rooms each. Each grouping of three housing units is considered to be a neighborhood. The rooms are very attractive, well-equipped, and can easily be individualized. Every room has a bed, chair, desk, and hanging area for clothes. The doors are solid wood with ventilation areas at the top and bottom. Each man has a key to his own room and each wing has its own dayroom with television and chairs. Outside is a patio which is excellent for lounging and table games including ping-pong.

Obviously the correctional philosophies represented by unit one at Vienna and the rest of that institution are worlds apart.

(3) In one region of the country, we visited two large institutions that served the same maximum security function—reception and classification. The planners of one of them decided that the type of prisoners served by a reception center demanded the most secure provisions for housing. Consequently, all cells are inside and wet. An inside cell is one with no external wall or no window. A wet cell is one that is self-contained as far as sanitary facilities are concerned. An inside wet cell thus provides no outside wall to breach, no window bars to cut, and its built-in sanitary facilities make unnecessary the opening of the grille cell door during hours when the custodial staff is spread thinly. Thus, in this insti-

tution, long two-tiered cellblocks securely confine over 800 men during most of the 30- to 45-day reception and classification period.

The planners of the other reception and classification center, which is in a nearby state but which deals with similar inmates, chose open wards located in widely separated buildings on a huge campus as the appropriate housing solution for the majority of its prisoners. This center has five dormitories housing over 800 inmates in open wards with little restriction of movement and only one building containing 138 single cells.

During our field trips we observed six basic types of living accommodations.

Types of Living Quarters

(1) Inside cells. We have already described these, but, to repeat, they have no outside wall or window. Usually they have sanitary facilities built in. The cell front almost invariably is of open grillwork thus providing maximum surveillance and minimum privacy. Inside cells are considered very secure and are very popular with custodial staff. They are also very expensive. They most certainly create a sensory experience marked by an inability to concentrate, read, or study, and in time a general state of withdrawal and autism.

(2) Outside cells or rooms. Outside cells are very much like inside cells except that they do have exterior walls and windows and are therefore considered easier to breach. The exterior window, however, provides better ventilation and light and infinitely more sensory stimulation. Most often, outside cells do not have open grille fronts, but their solid and secure doors do have observation panels. Privacy is considerable, but not total. Outside cells may be either wet or dry, that is, with or without self-contained sanitary facilities.

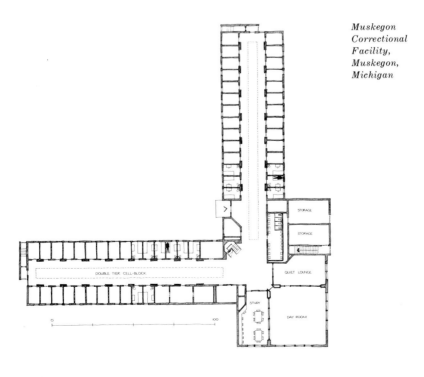

Muskegon Correctional Facility, Muskegon, Michigan

Rooms are not dramatically different from outside cells, but they usually have wooden doors to which, increasingly, the inmates possess keys. Rooms are less apt to contain toilets and usually do not have furniture that is fixed to the floor or walls. Rooms and outside cells that we saw measured between 60 and 110 square feet and were usually larger than inside cells.

(3) Segregation cells. These are special facilities built to contain and punish inmates presenting disciplinary problems. We saw several variations of the segregation cell. They will be discussed in a separate section.

(4) Squad rooms. These are small wards or large cells and may contain 4 to 8 beds. They are quite popular in county jails, and we have described them in the section on pretrial detention. However, we saw them in only one new correctional institution that we visited, the Federal Maximum Security Penitentiary at Marion, Illinois. They had originally been designed into that prison to house trusties who are now, however, being moved outside the walls where they live in new quarters. The officials at Marion would like very much to eliminate the squad rooms entirely. So would the inmates with whom we talked.

It should be noted that most correctional officials disapprove of two-man cells (though thousands of inmates presently are "doubled up") because of the opportunity for homosexuality. They also disapprove of three-man cells because sooner or later two occupants become "tight" at the expense of the third. Multiple occupancy cells, therefore, almost invariably provide for four or more occupants.

(5) Open wards or dormitories. The dormitory is one aspect of corrections on which both wardens and inmates agree. They both hate them. Yet economy, supported by the rationalizations published in handbooks dealing with correctional architecture, has ordained their existence. A very influential book on correctional architecture, for example, suggests that 62% of all prisoners be housed in open dormitories or in cubicles (these will be discussed later). It cites as advantages the lower construction costs, the greater flexibility (beds can be added or removed as population fluctuates), the reduced plumbing requirements, the ease of supervision, and then, compared to traditional steel and masonry cells, their less depressing appearance.

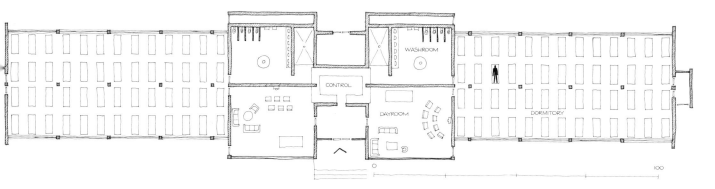

Reception and Medical Center, Lake Butler, Florida

With such persuasive arguments to support the open dormitory, it is not surprising that we saw many of them in correctional facilities for males of every security classification—minimum, medium, and maximum—and in institutions serving adults and juveniles. We saw none, however, in institutions for females. One commissioner for youth services with whom we talked argued that all boys should be housed in open wards ("they love them") and all girls in private rooms ("it is part of our culture"). Inasmuch as these statements came from an official in the deep South, we attributed his point of view to a chivalrously protective attitude toward the female. We are persuaded that open dormitories serve only one purpose. They are a way of making the construction budget stretch.

We observed several variations of open wards. A large medium security institution in California contained scores of relatively small wards, each designed for 16 men. These wards were built as part of two quadrangles, and their exterior walls provided much of the security of the center. Size was determined by the number of men to a work gang. Each housing unit contains at one end a dayroom that is used almost exclusively for television watching, which is the major correctional placebo. Most dayrooms are used in this way, as we have noted in the section of this book on recreation. At the other end is the bathroom. The most accessible entry to the ward is through the bathroom. As we were ushered through, our first view was of two men sitting on the "johns." They didn't seem to be embarrassed, but we were. Perhaps this is what some call the dehumanization process. We asked a group of inmates their appraisal of the dormitory. One replied, "We call them mixers." We asked why. His answer was, "In dormitories you mix youngsters with ignorance and oldsters with bitterness."

In a medium security institution in Colorado, we saw an unusual combination in which open wards and cells were side by side, part of the same living unit. The original plan, we were told, was to place the more aggressive and difficult men in the cells, the more tractable in the dormitories. In practice it has become just the opposite. The rooms are coveted and one earns his way into one. Misbehavior moves him out. As one black man said it, "Rooms are for men, man. Dormitories are for jitterbugs."

Many institutions that we visited contained both cells and open wards. Holman and Mt. Meigs in Alabama, Somers in Connecticut, Lake Butler in Florida, Bordentown in New Jersey, and the Marine Disciplinary Barracks at Camp Pendleton in California, all secure facilities, and the youth centers at Stockton in California and Tucson in Arizona, are examples.

Still other correctional centers contain open wards almost exclusively. Among them are Sierra in California, which we have already noted, Carson City, Nevada, and a host of boys' facilities such as Gatesville and Giddings in Texas and Skillman in New Jersey.

The Texas dormitories, we must note, are built to a design that provides surveillance during the night hours while allowing no opportunity for inmates to overpower the lone officer on duty. He is ensconced in an elevated observation room to which entrance can be made only via a secure outside door. The officer's role, during sleeping hours, is to observe. If intervention is required, reserve officers are summoned.

(6) Cubicles. These are compromises. They are less expensive to build than rooms and provide more privacy than open wards. Essentially they are made by partial walls built around a person's living space. We saw them used quite effectively in several different types of institutions including the Coastal Community Correctional Center in South Carolina, the new Women's Correctional Institution on Rikers Island in New York, and the excellent and very attractive girls' institutions at Macon, Georgia, and Waynesburg, Pennsylvania.

At Waynesburg, the cubicle is used to make more private and personal rooms which were built for four girls. A crosslike partition divides the large rooms into quadrants in which each girl has her bed, desk, dresser, individuality, and privacy.

The Robert F. Kennedy Youth Center in Morgantown, West Virginia, just a few miles from Waynesburg, also has

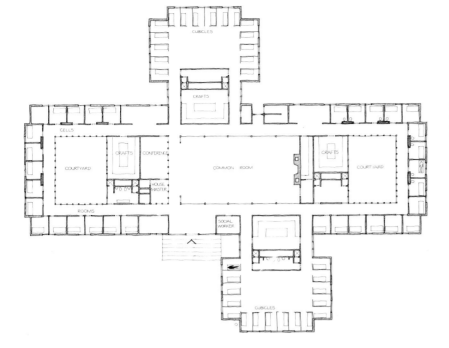

*Robert F. Kennedy
Youth Center,
Morgantown,
West Virginia*

cubicles. They are used as part of the behavioral modification program at that institution. This will be discussed in greater detail in a later chapter.

As noted earlier, security is a prime determinant of the basic shapes and forms of all correctional buildings, and housing facilities readily display their architectural indebtedness to control, surveillance, and security. The most dramatic example of this is undoubtedly the *Panopticon* housing unit in which hundreds of men in individual open grille cells can be constantly watched by one officer stationed in the center. The radial design, though rarely used any longer in total institutional design, still provides a series of options for housing units in institutions—even those which are basically of telephone pole or campus form. The radial design, of course, permits observation of several units from one location.

The massive five-, six-, and seven-tier cellblocks so common in older institutions are not being built today, but two and three floors of open galleries are still being constructed for both medium and maximum security purposes. Examples include the federal prison at Marion in Illinois and state institutions at Jackson in Georgia, Somers in Connecticut, Leesburg in New Jersey, Ionia in Michigan, Moberly in Missouri, and Canon City in Colorado. We saw no multitiered housing unit in any facility for either juveniles or women.

Less satisfactory from the standpoint of ease of observation but more suitable in many other aspects are those units which have substituted completely separate floors for the multilevel open tiers. These result in smaller, more discrete units offering better classification and treatment options and more noise abatement.

Institutions which we saw that utilized single-floor living units include Purdy in Washington, Kennedy in West Virginia, Fox Lake and Lincoln in Wisconsin, and institutions for youth at Waynesburg in Pennsylvania, Macon in Georgia, Echo Glen in Washington, and Tryon in New York. Multistoried buildings with discrete floors were the women's institutions in Canon City, Colorado, and Rikers Island, New York, and the institutions for men at Jamestown in California, Bordentown in New Jersey, and the 16-story high-rise facility at Morganton, North Carolina. The last named, like the Kennedy Center and others, has built a concept of treatment around the housing unit, and this warrants fuller description later in this chapter.

Other housing units that we saw were built in the form of squares, *H*'s, *U*'s, *L*'s, *E*'s, and *I*'s. One of the square-shaped housing units—that at Leesburg, New Jersey—is especially worthy of description.

Leesburg is a secure new prison designed to hold approximately 500 adult male felons. All living units are built around open courts, the four sides of which contain outside rooms built in two tiers. These rooms are self-contained and have secure, solid, prison-type doors which, like the rooms themselves, are painted in various hues. The inside wall of the housing square is glass from ceiling to floor almost giving the impression of no wall at all. The enclosed court is landscaped. One man, recently transferred from the ancient prison in Trenton, said that this was the first time in several years that he had the opportunity to observe the sky and trees.

Though most prisons which we visited were drab and grim and gave us the feeling that all of man's sensory needs had to be sacrificed to security and control in the prison setting, we found Leesburg architecturally different. So did the inmates and guards with whom we chatted. Only time will tell whether all the glass, colorful rooms, and landscaped gardens will survive the rigors of convict occupation. We hope they will.

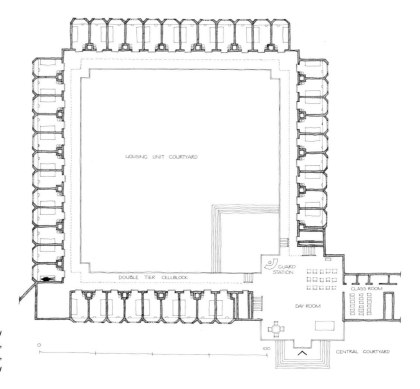

New Jersey State Prison, Leesburg, New Jersey

There is one additional form for living units that we saw. For the want of a better term, we call it modern collegiate, and it is not prisonlike at all. These units were not designed to insure surveillance, prevent destructiveness, control movement, or prevent escapes. They were designed simply to live in, and are common only to low security institutions. Some of the most attractive examples of these nonprisonlike housing units can be found at the juvenile institutions at Brownwood in Texas, Irma in Wisconsin, and Snoqualmie in Washington; the adult correctional centers at Vienna in Illinois and Fox Lake in Wisconsin; and the Purdy Women's Correctional Institution in Washington. This latter institution has housing features we saw nowhere else, including, adjacent to the main institution, a group of self-contained apartments. Girls who are ready for parole and prerelease programs live there. Each apartment has a kitchen, dinette, living room, two double bedrooms, and a bath. It is as homelike a setting as any correctional institution might ever be expected to provide.

Aside from their usual utilitarian functions, toilets and showers have been designed and located in many correctional institutions to serve three additional purposes: to ease surveillance, to prevent undesired prisoner mobility, and to withstand punishment.

Sanitary Facilities

The designers of most correctional institutions for men have decided to forfeit privacy which they obviously consider of lesser value, for ease of observation which they consider to be of great importance. As a result, showers and toilets in most institutions for men are pretty much out in the open. Toilets in cells were usually located immediately inside the open grilles or where they were observable through the glazed panels of solid doors. In dormitories, toilets were also usually very exposed and often not separated from the bed area.

Toilets were also frequently located in cells, dormitories, dayrooms, and recreation and work areas to reduce the occasion for inmate mobility. Cell toilets, for example, rendered unnecessary the opening and closing of cell doors especially at night when staff complements are usually low. Open sanitary facilities in shops and dayrooms enable detail officers to keep all of their charges under constant observation.

Institutions for girls and women are apparently exempted from the conditions described above. We invariably found that women's institutions provided toilet and shower stalls. Wet rooms were usually restricted to the admission and disciplinary areas. In the correctional milieu, personal privacy is apparently important only to the female.

Dayrooms　　Dayrooms have increasingly become important elements of the housing units. No longer is it common to lock men or women in their rooms during nonworking hours. Increasingly, institutions provide a wide range of recreational, hobby, and self-help activities for the leisure time hours. Dayrooms allow for recreational and group activities.

The dayrooms that we saw varied enormously. Some were nothing more than wide spaces between two banks of cells where men or women might sit and play cards or watch television. Others, shaped more like rooms, were nevertheless austerely, even uncomfortably, furnished and offered a minimum of space for table games and television.

Vast empty corridors often serve as dayrooms.

The dayrooms at some institutions were designed to provide comfortable and attractive space for casual activities. Leesburg and Fox Lake are among the more secure facilities in attractive settings. Dayrooms there, as in so many other places, have unfortunately become little theaters for televiewing. Two institutions, the Robert F. Kennedy Center at Morgantown and the Michigan Training Unit at Ionia, provide two dayrooms in each housing unit—one for television and one for other activities. In these two places, television does not have to be the inmate's only choice.

Extraordinary living room facilities are provided at Purdy, the Women's Correctional Center in Washington, and at several juvenile facilities, especially Brownwood in Texas, Irma in Wisconsin, Snoqualmie in Washington, and Waynesburg in Pennsylvania. Some of these feature fireplaces, ample area for dancing, ping-pong and pool tables, comfortable furniture, and most imaginative design. They serve as places where staff, friends, residents, and families interact under pleasant conditions.

It should be noted, in several institutions which we visited, that dining was an extra function of the dayroom area, but we will discuss the whole matter of food service later in this book.

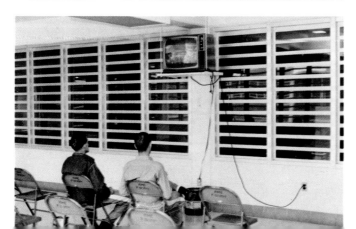

The Housing Unit and Treatment

Treatment facilities will be described later in this book, but it is important to note now that in increasing numbers of institutions—adult as well as juvenile—the housing unit is becoming central to the treatment process. Most juvenile administrators have moved toward decentralizing authority, discipline, and counseling down to the cottage unit. From an architectural point of view, therefore, space must be available in the living quarters for individual counseling, group interaction, and case management. Many new institutions do not have such facilities in their housing units, and the treatment effort, therefore, has suffered. Official after official bemoaned the fact that such provisions had not been made at the design stage.

Even in adult prisons, classification teams are being assigned to separate housing areas in an effort to reduce the megaprison to manageable treatment units. Generally, those plants do not provide office and counseling space for these important activities. In some instances, cell space has been converted to treatment purposes; in others, dayrooms have been removed from other uses. Warden after warden suggested that counseling and group treatment space be a part of every housing unit. One official was very annoyed because, for a reason beyond understanding, the counseling office had been placed in the administrative building outside of the security perimeter. It was inaccessible to all but a few trusted inmates.

In two operating institutions and in the plans of one that is under construction, we saw housing being used as part of the reward system of sophisticated behavior modification programs, and this will be discussed in greater detail later. We note now, however, that at the Kennedy Youth Center at Morgantown, West Virginia, each housing unit has three qualities of sleeping space. A new inmate begins in a cubicle for which he pays a minimal "rent." As his trustworthiness and "income" rises, he may go into a private room with modest furnishings. Still later, he may achieve even more comfortable private quarters.

The Western North Carolina Correctional Center in Morganton is a 16-story high-rise. The top floor is reserved for behavioral problems, the 15th for reception, and the next several floors for inmate housing. Each subsequently lower floor has improved furnishings and equipment. For example, the 14th floor might be Spartanlike; the 13th adds a radio; the 12th a television; the 11th a ping-pong table, etc. Food is served in the housing unit, and service improves as one moves up (down, that is) the behavior modification scale.

The federal government is planning to open a new facility at Camp Butner, North Carolina, and it apparently will operate similarly.

What has emerged from our analysis of correctional housing are a few principles which we feel are worth summarizing.

• *The tremendous inconsistencies we saw between institutions ostensibly housing similar populations make us conclude that planners do not attempt to relate security accommodations to the security needs of the incarcerated. The examples of security "overkill" that we saw demonstrated financial waste as well as inefficiency.*

• *The total impact of the correctional experience is determined by other elements in combination with the type of housing. Therefore, the physical aspects of housing must be viewed along with program involvement, staffing patterns, inspection policies, and a whole host of nonphysical elements. Quite simply, if a man feels he is being helped by participation in a program and gets support and reinforcement from staff, he is likely to tolerate the barest of adequate quarters. In Chino's Palm Hall, for example, inmate after inmate confided extremely positive attitudes toward their experience at that facility. The physical facility was hardly plush, and in fact was stark. The old chestnut about being able to run a good correctional program in an old red barn is admittedly too simplistic, and we do not subscribe to any housing that doesn't meet standards of care and concern. The point is, however, that the acceptability of an institution, and hence the effect of it on an inmate, is determined by sociological and psychological attitudes as well as the mere provision of physical amenities.*

• *The above leads us to state that any attempt to design better institutions or to make cosmetic modifications of housing facilities cannot suffice of itself as the means to change men any more than a new school building insures an improvement in the education process therein. The entire context of the process must be examined, and, even more fundamentally, the use of the institution as a corrective vehicle needs validation.*

Segregation

In all the highly secure institutions and in many of the reduced custody ones, we found special sections that were, in effect, prisons within prisons. They are called by many names—punitive segregation, administrative quarantine, adjustment unit, Siberia, the Box, the Klondike, and most frequently the Hole. Whatever they are called their purposes are to punish misbehavior and/or separate difficult inmates from the general population. Interestingly enough, they exist for the same reasons that their host, the prison, exists—because we cannot tolerate deviant behavior. In the world outside, the ordinary inhabitants demand that offenders be punished. In the world inside, the ordinary inhabitants—inmates and line staff—make the same demand. During my 11 years as cochairman of the disciplinary board of a New Jersey correctional institution, the pressure to "lock them up" came not only from guards who wanted their authority respected and enforced, but also from inmates who wanted protection from theft, assault, and rape. In that time I was responsible for over 30,000 disciplinary decisions, including over 2,000 to place men in segregation. You can believe me, that was a sobering experience.

The disciplinary process within the correctional institution is more arbitrary and capricious, by far, than the system outside. Sometimes the complainant is an informer, and he never faces the accused before the "court line" or "adjustment committee" or "disciplinary board." More often he is an officer who may or may not be objective and fair. Nevertheless the officer's accusation is usually tantamount to a finding of guilt, for it is a correctional precept that the officer's word must be upheld. Even the fairly simple offenses, like fighting, are almost impossible to adjudicate. Each participant passionately denies that he initiated the trouble. Because witnesses are almost never called and cross-examinations are very rare, determining who is culpable is most difficult. A standard response is to treat the two as equally guilty; to say weakly, "It takes two to tango," and lock up both participants.

Especially difficult inmates may be segregated without specific offense or hearing for months or even years simply because they are active in prison politics, homosexuality, escape prone, or just plain ornery. In short, due process has not had a significant place in that most autocratic of American institutions, the prison.

Justice in a prison is a very ugly microcosm of society's criminal justice practices. In the outside community, we hope that fear of imprisonment will control man's more negative impulses. We call it deterrence. Yet the crime rate is intolerably high. Likewise in the prison, we expect that fear of the Hole will deter men from unruly behavior, yet the crime rate within the prisons — larcenies, muggings, sexual assaults, gambling, and the rest — is undoubtedly even higher than in the free community. From time to time at Bordentown we would escort a newly admitted inmate who had a bad reputation to the segregation unit and show him the stark punishment cells void of furniture, with only a hole in the floor to serve as a toilet. Thick iron doors closed the small cells off from sound or light. Yet, more often than not, that very inmate would in a short time be in one of those cells.

When deterrence has failed and a man is sent to prison, the public expects that confinement will in some mysterious way "teach him a lesson" or "reform him." But generally it doesn't. An ever-growing percentage of all street crime is committed by men who have known imprisonment and have been embittered rather than reformed by it. Likewise within the prison, most of the offenses continue to be committed by the same individuals who have, over and over again, experienced the dehumanizing effects of punitive segregation. To change human nature apparently requires less simplistic solutions than the prison or the Hole, but apparently we don't know what those solutions might be. We remain dependent upon old and ugly techniques.

The segregation units that we saw ranged from the totally unacceptable to the barely tolerable. In one prison the Hole was actually a hole—a cave dug into the side of a quarry. It is still there for all to see. In it the most intractable inmates were, until recently, confined. One, an American Indian, with whom we talked, had been so uncontrollable that he had been kept in that hole for years. Inmate after inmate told us, and officials did not deny it, that his cell door had been welded closed. Eventually, a new warden abolished the use of the cave and the Indian was released. But by this time he had become blind. That was in an old prison, but we saw uncivilized practices in some of the newest.

Different institutions obviously used these segregation cells in different ways, and some places apparently were more humane than others. It is in the segregation unit that American penology reaches its ugliest depths. There, the brute hostility of the inmate confronts the primitive authority of the correctional establishment.

In one institution at the time of our survey, nearly 18% of the inmate population was in some kind of segregation— 19 in isolation, 65 in segregation, and an additional 35 in a disciplinary quarantine, flatteringly called the "halfway house." The isolation was especially brutal. As many as eight people have been locked into one of the tiny, dark, airless, and bedless isolation cells for up to 21 days. During our visit these gloomy, bare dungeons contained two, three, and four men sitting naked on the floors. Only the 5-inch holes in the floors, used as toilets, served any human purpose.

The 19 men in the isolation cells were being punished for such diverse offenses as fighting, possessing homemade knives, drinking "julep," and refusing to be transferred from a cell to a dormitory. One man had broken up his cell furniture. His succinct explanation as shown on the disciplinary report was, "I'm tired of this fucking place." Autistic, hallucinating, and psychotic behavior, as well as other serious forms of pathology, are not uncommon.

When we left that sad, sad prison we were reminded of Primo Levi, speaking of his experiences at Auschwitz in *If This Is Man:*

> *It is not possible to sink lower than this; no human condition is more miserable than this, nor could it be conceivably so. Nothing belongs to us anymore; they have taken away our clothes, our shoes, even our hair; if we speak, they will not listen to us, and if they listen, they will not understand.*

Most new ones, however, are less totally intolerable—at least from the physical point of view. Fairly typical for a

large maximum security prison is the segregation-quarantine unit of the federal penitentiary at Marion, Illinois. It is a two-story cellhouse containing four blocks of 18 inside cells. Half of the cells are used for administrative quarantine. In a large prison system there always seems to be a number of persons who, for one reason or another, must be removed from the general population for extended periods— sometimes even permanently. There are inmates, for example, who have been witnesses against others and who require extremely close supervision because of constant threat to their lives. Others have habits or mannerisms that are so effeminate and flamboyant that they are dangerously disruptive. It is tragic that, in the unisex environment of this prison, passions over another man can become so explosive. Some prisoners are unalterably committed to escape, and others are chronically and dangerously assaultive. Recently many institutions have had a new kind of problem inmate—the activist. Many administrators have arbitrarily decided to isolate him from the general population. The administrative quarantine area serves the purpose of severely restricting movement of these people. The cells are nearly identical to the inside cells in the rest of the prison. Each contains a bed, chair, desk, and a combination water closet-sink made of metal. An extremely wide corridor along the face of the cells is designed to provide space for group recreation. But because serious disturbances have occurred in that area, group activities have been discontinued. Men are allowed out of their cells for exercise one at a time.

The other half of the unit, 36 cells in all, is used for punitive segregation. Men are assigned to it for relatively short periods as punishment for specific acts of misbehavior. Half of the 36 segregation cells are similar to those in the quarantine area described above. The other 18 are in one cellblock and have been specially designed to contain those explosive prisoners likely to act in an aggressive or destructive manner. This block contains a small unit of 8 ultrasecure detention rooms. These have the sparsest furniture, toilets designed to be unbreakable (though they are not), and solid iron doors. It should be noted that the Federal Bureau of Prisons has refused to permit "French toilets"—the hole in the floor type—in this maximum security prison.

The wide corridor on this cellblock is divided by grillwork to prevent exercising prisoners from having any direct physical contact with those in the cells. On the far side of the grille, a small area contains equipment including non-moving bicycles, weights, and rowing-type apparatus. These, of course, help men keep in shape, but, more importantly, enable them to burn up energies that might otherwise explode during their confinement.

The segregation cellblocks at Marion are immediately adjacent to the recreation yards and this, officials say, is unfortunate for at least two reasons. Men inside from time to time feign brutality, we were told, screaming as if they were being beaten or tortured. These sounds can be heard by prisoners during recreation periods and cause bitterness and unrest among the general population. In most prisons nontruths become widely accepted as truths. Mutual trust between inmates and staff has never been an attribute of the closed institution. Secondly, unauthorized communication between the segregation units and the general population is almost impossible to control. A new segregation unit is therefore planned. It will have no outside windows.

Other maximum security prisons that we visited have segregation units more or less similar to those described above. The principal characteristics are remoteness from the main part of the institution, inside cells, minimal or no furniture, doors made of grilles and/or solid iron panels, indestructible-type toilet-sinks or French-type toilets, the flushing of which is controlled by the officer outside the cell. In some places that we visited this flushing was deliberately repeated at regular intervals throughout the day and night, adding to the unpleasantness of the segregation experience.

Several reduced custody institutions were on our itinerary and, as might be expected, their segregation sections were not so large or forbidding. Essentially there are two reasons for this. The selection process by which men are assigned to reduced custody facilities usually weeds out the most troublesome inmates. And secondly, should the selection process err, the unruly one can be, and is, transferred to a more secure prison.

The medium security institutions at Canon City, Colorado, Carson City, Nevada, Fox Lake, Wisconsin, and Ionia, Michigan, for example, are all located within reasonable distance of the maximum security prisons in the respective states. None of these institutions has more than a very few segregation cells. While we were at Carson City we did witness a summary transfer of a man back "to the walls." The captain in charge of that medium security institution said he would not be able to run it if the threat of the "walls" was removed.

Leesburg, New Jersey, and Sierra, California, are two medium security institutions that are not located close to maximum security facilities. Originally Sierra, which has all open wards, had no special provisions for segregation. Jerry-built arrangements have since been provided, but Sierra must still resort to transfer for the very troublesome inmates. Leesburg, unlike Sierra, has all individual rooms and no open wards. Minor problem makers are restricted to their quarters and there are eight disciplinary cells adjacent to the hospital. Incidentally, several wardens told us that all segregation units should be adjacent to hospitals to insure greater ease in providing the medical examinations and observation required for disturbed inmates as well as more immediate emergency treatment.

The disciplinary areas of most of the new women's institutions that we visited are less dismal than those in men's institutions. There are four isolation cells at Salem, Oregon, but an administrative decision has kept them out of use. In Purdy, Washington, and Rikers Island, New York, the isolation rooms are similar in size, shape, and furnishings to the general housing units, except that they contain toilets and sinks, thus reducing the necessity for frequent opening and closing of doors. At Canon City, Colorado, the segregation unit is on a lower level adjacent to the hospital. Its rooms are similar in design to the segregation cells of institutions for men. On the first day of our visit an unfortunate incident occurred. Because of overcrowding in the reception area a new admission was placed in a segregation cell — an experience that might bring despair to even an old prison hand. The new arrival set her mattress on fire. Girls became sick from inhalation. There was considerable smoke and water damage. Staff were excited and very busy responding to the emergency, and the entire inmate population was very shaken. Rumors spread far more rapidly than the mattress flames.

Disciplinary problems are, of course, not limited to adult corrections. Young offenders can be difficult too. Most of the juvenile institutions that we saw are more positively oriented than adult institutions. They provide better staff to child ratios, richer relationships, and more extensive programming. As a result, punitive segregation is resorted to much less frequently.

In Texas, for example, a complex of schools for juvenile delinquents holds over 2,000 boys almost exclusively in open wards. There are, in all but one of the four units visited, no individual sleeping rooms and no rooms specifically for isolation. There is a unit for 400 of the more difficult and escape-minded lads and it has a fence around it. The other units do not have fences. But, like these other units, its sleeping quarters, with one exception, are open wards. The exception is a 40-bed segregation unit containing two wings of 20 rooms each. These rooms are not stripped of furniture and they do contain toilets and sinks. One of the two wings is no longer used for segregation. It has been converted to a classroom for instruction in data processing. On the night of our unannounced visit there were only six boys (out of 2,000) occupying the remaining segregation unit — four for fighting, one for attempt to escape, and one for making what was interpreted to be an improper advance to one of the young pretty miniskirted clerks. Since our visit the situation may have changed. We read of a court action in which the Texas Youth Council is accused of brutal practices in its segregation units.

In other new juvenile institutions visited, one "quiet room" for every 15 to 20 youngsters seemed the rule, but most often these were unoccupied. At the Federal Youth

Center at Morgantown, West Virginia, an institution designed for a maximum of 325 young offenders, 12 rooms are provided for segregation. We noted that those assigned to the segregation unit participated in congregate activities during the day. In fact, we had a very informative gripe session with the five young men who were in that unit on one of the days of our visit. Three, I recollect, were awaiting federal court action for escape.

Morganton, North Carolina, a very new youth center, has a fairly large and dismal segregation unit. It can hardly be called the Hole because it is located on the 16th floor of this high-rise facility located in the foothills of the Smokies. It must be said that Morganton was originally intended to be a very secure facility for adults. Its assigned purpose was changed after construction was well under way. The present administration plans a very intense behavior modification program there. Consequently the superintendent does not view this secure segregation unit as an instrument of punishment. Rather he sees it primarily as a place where young offenders can act out their problems and hostilities without hurting themselves or anyone else. For this purpose, the 16th floor provides 33 prison-type inside cells, each with built-in steel bed, table and chair, unbreakable toilet, and open grilles. It also has three segregation cells with unbreakable toilets and solid security doors. Finally there are two isolation cells with solid security doors and French-type toilets in the floor.

Until recently neither the legislature nor the judicial branch of government would interfere with this autocracy bestowed upon the correctional bureaucrats. Judges did not, for example, question the indiscriminate use of "lock-up" facilities such as we have described. Recent court decisions throughout the country now give clear indication that the correctional system must function within the framework of the Constitution. Judges are demanding that an administrator present more than a vague justification for punishment before denying a man freedom within the correctional setting. In serious cases, courts have demanded that officials provide the trappings of "due process" including a hearing before an impartial board, the right to answer charges, to cross-examine the accuser, and to present witnesses. These courts have also challenged the constitutionality of some segregation units calling upon the prohibitions against cruel and unusual punishment of the Eighth Amendment.

In short, the correctional institution is being brought closer to the mainstream of American values. Its managers will have to find different methods for dealing with institutional problems. Most certainly the intolerable segregation facilities and practices described above will not be acceptable much longer.

America still has more than its share of old prisons in which men eat monotonous institutional cooking under conditions totally void of personal choice, pleasant surroundings, or companionable associations. We saw some of them. They have row upon row of backless benches and tables all facing one direction. Men march silently to their respective places and sit mutely staring at the back of the heads of the men in front. Such mess halls are huge, drab, hot, noisy, and very regimented. Some have catwalks from which armed guards maintain close scrutiny. In others, elevated control rooms have slots from which tear gas and, if need be, bullets can be sprayed upon disorderly prisoners. If there is any fear that preoccupies prison managers from coast to coast, it is fear of disorder in the dining room. Consequently knives or even forks may be banned because they might be used as weapons. Condiments such as salt and pepper are missing from the table for fear that they might be tossed into the eyes of guards. Tables and benches alike are solidly fastened to the floor.

Food Services

congregate dining in close proximity to cells

Carved into the mantelpiece of the dining room of the old Horn mansion in Philadelphia are the words, "It is good to be merry with meat." Such advice never reached the operators of many of our old prisons and, sadly, is not reaching some of the new correctional administrators either. On the other hand, it must be said that architects are recently designing much more pleasant environments for dining (which many correctional people perhaps accurately call "feeding," as in feeding animals).

As is true of all components of a correctional facility, con-

trol is a basic determinant of the design of the dining room. The food service facility of an institution for intractable offenders differs immensely from the dining room of an open campus for delinquent children. But even among institutions having similar security classifications, we saw wide differences in the quality of the dining environment.

We observed two basic types of eating arrangements—central and scattered—plus variations of each.

Central dining is common to all noncampus type institutions that we visited and to most large ones, including those of campus design. Men and women, regardless of their work, treatment, or housing assignments, recess to one central dining room for their meals. Generally the food is prepared in the same "food service" building where it is served.

In the new maximum security prisons that we visited, this central dining room is located within the most secure area of the institution, usually within sight and sound of the prison's control center. It is designed to provide maximum visual observation and good control of movement. Cafeteria-type serving is universal, with the resulting lengthy lines so abhorrent to those of us who served as enlisted personnel.

The room itself is usually, but not always, severe in design with hard masonry and metal finishes and harsh lights. Tables are heavy, often of stainless steel, and fastened securely to the floor. Backless stools, which we found to be intolerably uncomfortable, are welded to crossarms that are themselves welded to the central leg of the table. Some of these tables seat as many as ten, but the four-man table was almost universal in the prisons that we visited. The tables are lined in monotonous precision. In the new maximum security prisons that we visited we found only two exceptions. At Somers in Connecticut, the tables are similar to those already described except that variety in the form of two-, four-, or six-man tables is provided. At Marion, the federal institution that was designed to replace the ultrasecure Alcatraz, comfortable and movable chairs and tables make a lie of the assertion that such amenities are impossible in a secure prison setting.

Almost invariably the dining rooms that we saw were designed to seat only part of the institution's population, thus maximizing use of space and at the same time reducing the numbers assembled at any one moment. I have mentioned that wardens, out of experience, fear disorder in the dining room. It is natural, then, for them to want to keep the crowds small. One new maximum security prison in Alabama, for example, has a dining room so small that it can serve only one-eighth of the men at one seating. Thus the number seated at any one time is kept small, but dining there has become a rushed, irritating, and continuous process from dawn to dusk. It was not uncommon to find scheduling that required a man to have supper at 4:00 p.m. and then to go without food until 7:30 next morning.

Several institutions that have central food services have responded to the problems of bigness by dividing the dining room in two, thus reducing the size of the crowds, and aslo the noise, which in most prisons that we visited was unbearable.

The Youth Development Center for Girls at Waynesburg, Pennsylvania, has one central food service facility, but it is partitioned by attractive dividers into a series of small dining rooms each providing comfortable dining space for the girls and staff from each cottage. In most of the institutions we visited, the staff dined in facilities separate from the inmates.

The central dining rooms of many of the reduced custody institutions are imaginative. Frequently, they are the central accent of the entire facility design. Leesburg, a medium custody prison in New Jersey, is a notable example. This is not a campus-type institution; all buildings adjoin each other. However, there are no corridors. Courtyards serve as avenues for all movement. The food service building rises high above all the rest of the complex. The ground level is open and is a natural extension of the main courtyard of the institution. Men enter the dining area via a ramp that winds up from the ground level and leave by a second ramp at the other end, thus eliminating the traffic problem we observed in many other places. The dining room itself has an extraordinarily high ceiling that gives a feeling of space and seems to dissipate heat and noise. One entire wall of the building, equivalent to three stories in height, is glass, thus providing the unusual sense of openness. This whole adventurous design is somewhat spoiled by the same prison tables that were objectionable to us in the more dreary prisons that we visited. Despite some of the more positive aspects of this design, these fixed tables and the room's enormous scale add up to the same old mass "feeding" concept.

Several campus-type correctional facilities including those at Fox Lake, Wisconsin; Ionia, Michigan; Vienna, Illinois; and Morgantown, West Virginia have bright and attractive dining rooms, and they, like Leesburg, feature much glass. Because so much of my correctional experience was in a very secure facility with minimal glass, I found this change not only pleasant but a little unbelievable.

At Morgantown I asked officers and inmates alike about breakage. I was sure that the young active fellows at this federal youth center would have a ball, especially in view of the fact that the entire food service building is bordered with four feet of river rocks. But at the time of our visit only one panel had been broken—by a visiting professor who walked through it.

Inmates at Leesburg had an interesting theory about all the glass there. These inmates, it should be noted, had just been transferred to the new prison from the ancient and intolerable old dungeons at Trenton and Rahway. They said, "All that glass improves guard-inmate relations." I asked,

"How?" The reply, "A guard can't stay on my back or I'll kick out all the glass." Interesting theory! At any rate the officers thought the inmates behaved better and the inmates thought the guards were more tolerable. Both gave the credit to the design and all that glass.

The planners of juvenile institutions frequently have been willing to sacrifice the economy of mass feeding for the many advantages of scattered dining rooms for small groups. Lincoln, Wisconsin, and Echo Glen, Washington, in our view, provide notable examples of attractive dining rooms for small groups within the housing units. Here, as in most of the institutions utilizing small group dining, the food is prepared in a central kitchen and delivered in hot carts to the various dining rooms.

We saw difficulties with scattered dining. The MacDougall Youth Development Center in South Carolina, for example, has recently given up scattered in favor of central dining. The reason for the change there is unusual. The trainlike steam carts require hard-surfaced paths connecting the central kitchen with the cottages and they are not available. Morgantown was also designed to permit dining in the housing units but has opted for a central eating arrangement.

Many juvenile institutions enjoy the best of both worlds. In Texas, for example, at both Giddings (boys) and Brownwood (girls) the students follow a schedule similar to that which they would at home. They have breakfast and dinner in their living unit where there is a full kitchen and pleasant eating space. They take lunch in the cafeteria of the school at the institution. Skillman in New Jersey has a similar arrangement. In the attractively designed school for girls in Macon, Georgia, most meals are served in a central facility. Each cottage, however, has a small kitchen for snacks and weekend meals. Echo Glen and Purdy, both handsomely designed and both in the state of Washington, have similar accommodations.

The provisions for dining at the brand new youth center at Morganton, North Carolina, warrant special note. Morganton is a high-rise of 16 stories. There is no central dining room. Food is served in multipurpose rooms that are located on each housing floor. These same rooms double as dayrooms and school rooms and are actively used 16 hours a day. Morganton's program is highly structured around behavior modification principles and this will be discussed in a subsequent chapter. It is important to report here, however, that dining is part and parcel of the behavior modification format.

One starts his residency at Morganton on one of the upper floors where the food service is extremely austere. As his behavior "modifies," he progresses downward. Each subsequent lower floor provides increased comforts, condiments, and utensils until, on the lowest housing unit, he has tablecloths, full silverware, and real china. The theory, of course, is to introduce a system of rewards into the correctional process which in the past has depended almost exclusively on negative sanctions to control behavior.

The kitchen at Morganton is on the second floor, and it was designed as the food preparation center for all the correctional camps and institutions in western North Carolina. Plans have changed and now it will be used only to prepare food for the youth center. It will also be central to a vocational program through which the superintendent hopes to develop gourmet cooks for the restaurant industry.

Its kitchen is massive and, in my opinion, oversize and overequipped for its purpose. This, perhaps, can be explained by the change that we have noted in the kitchen's function. However, we suspect that the food equipment salesmen are the most persuasive people in the world with the possible exception of those people who make and sell prison hardware. Not only at Morganton, but at Morgantown, Jackson, and in many institutions that we visited, we found kitchens which, according to their own food service supervisors, were equipped for three to five times the population to be served.

I suppose there is no place in the world where food service holds higher importance than in the correctional institution. There are at least two reasons for this. First and foremost the inmate has no option, if he wants to eat at all, than to eat the food served in the dining facility provided. He can't break the monotony by stopping off at the Four Seasons or even MacDonald's for something different. Secondly, inmates frequently have problems with authority. For them, a drab, regimented, and untasty eating experience three times a day, ad infinitum, becomes a focal point of and contributor to their hostility — even hate. Food, its preparation, and the surroundings in which it is partaken, are all of paramount significance.

Religion

From the beginning of the penitentiary in America, religion has been viewed as a most important part of the inmate's experience in prison. In fact, the designers of the legendary Eastern State Penitentiary saw three benefits in the solitude of its cells: (1) the felon was separated from the evil influences of the outside world; (2) he could overcome his indolence through hard labor at his work bench; and (3) he could read the Scriptures and find in them the principles of right and wrong that could change his ways. We have already noted that at Eastern only selected persons could serve as "prison visitors" to break the awful solitude of the prison's cells. These visitors were almost exclusively religious persons who brought with them piety and religious tracts.

The first noncustodial persons to be regularly employed in correctional institutions were chaplains, and years ago in penal institutions the issue of possible conflict with the principle of "separation of church and state" was resolved by the courts. They have consistently held that, because of the involuntary restriction on movement inherent in imprisonment, the state must provide all reasonable assistance to the inmate in the practice of his faith.

Traditionally this has meant that Protestant, Catholic, and Jewish chaplains have been provided, full- or part-time, depending upon the size of the institutions and the religious persuasions of the inmate populations. Recently there has been a remarkable increase in the number of offenders identifying with other religions or sects—most notably Muslims and Buddhists. Correctional administrators have been slow in providing for the religious needs of these groups, often responding only under pressure of court orders. This resistance on the part of officials to recognize emerging religious concepts and forms is unfortunate, it seems to us. A basic reason for all religions—for their being—is that they give strength and guidance to the downtrodden in their time of need. It should be expected, therefore, that prisons be the spawning grounds of new religious beliefs, and they are.

Our study team was composed of persons with strong positive identifications with organized religion. One served for years as an elder of his church. Another is a leader and officer in his synagogue. A third studied for the Roman Catholic priesthood. But as a group we were distressed at the amount of money that has been put into the construction of chapels in many of our newer correctional facilities.

An example of this is the youth complex at Stockton, California. It was built for 1,200 lads, and actually held at the time of our visit less than 800; yet there are six handsome chapels, three Catholic and three Protestant, all elegant and completely equipped. Any one of them would serve magnificently an outside community of several hundred people.

Though Stockton is extreme, many of the major new institutions that we visited had two chapels, one designated for Catholics, one for Protestants. They were often identical structures and usually side by side. Probably the most expensive and interesting, from a design point of view, are the twin chapels at the Illinois minimum security penitentiary at Vienna, Illinois. This imaginatively designed campus-type institution has at its hub a "town square" containing its school, library, gymnasium, and a series of small shops. The central accent of the entire campus are two handsome chapels and a single bell tower. Each chapel contains, in addition to the sanctuary, classroom space for church-related activities. All of this was very impressive but, to us, unconscionably wasteful. The large Catholic chapel, in which pews had not yet been installed, contained 12 temporary seats huddled together near the communion rail. The rest of the sanctuary was starkly bare. We were told that the Catholic church-going population at Vienna on any Sunday thus far had not overtaxed the 12 temporary chairs.

More satisfactory to us were the multifaith chapels which we saw in many institutions including the federal facilities at Morgantown, West Virginia and Marion, Illinois; the State Penitentiary at Somers, Connecticut; the youth correction centers at Yardville, New Jersey and Camp Hill, Pennsylvania; the Girls' School at Brownwood, Texas; and at several other locations. These were all chapels built exclusively for religious functions, but they were designed to accommodate suitably the Catholic, the Protestant, and, in some cases, the Jewish services. Rotating pulpits, for example, provided for the varying liturgical requirements.

The chapel at the Robert F. Kennedy Youth Center at Morgantown, West Virginia, warrants special description. The Kennedy Center is a campus-type facility in which the buildings, scattered around attractively landscaped acres, are connected by curving walkways. A winding stream and a lake add beauty. In the center of this handsome campus, and forming its focal point, is the Chapel of the Ark. Its curving roof complements the surrounding hills as it sweeps upward. Inside, softly colored glass, rich woodwork, sloping floor, and curving ceiling all add to its unique beauty. Residents and staff consider it inspirational. It is probably more opulent than most churches built in our newer suburbs, but it does not seem out of place at the Kennedy Center which is by no means an underfinanced physical facility. We did not feel that the Chapel of the Ark was the hypocritical religious structure that so many chapels appeared to us to be, because the other physical resources at Morgantown were of comparable beauty and utility.

Chapel of the Ark

Many religious structures were built, we were convinced, to impress the public and the legislators much more than to serve the needs of the prisoners. Those chapels were the starting point for most official tours. "See that lovely chapel! Aren't we doing great things for our criminals?" seemed to be their basic purpose. This was especially true in those facilities that were devoid of elementary program space. We visited one institution in which the dining room, used three times daily, doubled as a gymnasium and was in demand all day and all evening. Yet across the corridor was a chapel utilized only two hours a week by a mere handful of men, and it was locked tight the rest of the week. The inmates viewed this as the height of hypocrisy. They told us that the chapel primarily served the needs of the ultra-religious former warden who designed it. In still another very large prison serving nearly 2,000 offenders who were mostly young, we found no inside space for recreation or physical activities. But there was a huge, new, pretentious chapel. An inmate told me that its presence was enough to turn him against organized religion.

Other inmates complained to us of the perverted uses of religion in correctional institutions. In some, for example, church attendance records were taken, recorded, and made available to the parole boards. Thus, men attended church in order to accumulate "brownie points." In fairness, we must note that inmates participate in other programs—school, therapy, work—for the same reason. The Quakers in *Struggle for Justice*, their critique of contemporary corrections, put it this way: There is "a general consensus of inmates and staff that inmates must participate in treatment programs in order to be paroled. The undisguised cynicism they exhibit implies that the programs are regarded as phony and that the motivation for participation is to manipulate the parole process."

We were impressed by those institutions in which the religious facilities were designed to serve multiple purposes. The women's prison in Colorado, for example, has an all-purpose room with pulpits recessed behind rich, red drapes. The design of the room provides a reverent atmosphere when it is serving as a chapel, yet its flexibility allows it to be used for a variety of other desirable group activities.

We recognize the symbolic importance in corrections of having facilities designed exclusively for the worship of God. But we also observed as we toured the country that most correctional institutions seriously lack the space needed to permit a range of constructive activity throughout the waking day. It seems to us that the planners of our correctional institutions must learn a lesson from our colleges and communities. A recent study of 100 colleges, for example, revealed that their chapels were the least used and often the most expensive buildings on campus. University officials, in this time of tight money, feel the obligation to maximize the use of all campus facilities. They are, therefore, seeking ways to increase flexibility in the use of these chapels. The same is true in many American communities. It is no longer easy to raise sufficient money to build new churches and temples in which the sanctuary is designed only for formal services. Many, therefore, are built to provide for the multiple activities that the modern congregation requires. To those of us who were taught that "where two or three are gathered together in My name, there I will be also," such flexibility seems in no way irreverent.

A student of America once wrote:

Recreation

The several American states preserve their individual independence, and each of them is sovereign master to rule itself according to its own pleasure. By the side of one state, the penitentiaries of which might serve as a model, we find another whose prisons present the example of everything which ought to be avoided.

Those words might have been written today rather than fourteen decades earlier when Alexis de Tocqueville and Gustave de Beaumont toured American prisons in search of a model for a new penology for France. The contrasts in recreational facilities in the contemporary correctional institutions that we visited revealed the worst and the best, as de Tocqueville observed, in states that are side by side.

In one state, for example, we visited a reception and classification center that was first opened as recently as January, 1970. On the day of our visit, it held 440 felons most of whom had just been received into the state's correctional system from the courts. This is a compact, very secure, and highly automated institution with banks of television monitors substituting for face-to-face supervision by an officer. This institution was built to perform one function — to warehouse men at the lowest possible per capita cost during the periods necessary for reception, classification, and medical care. At this institution there are no dayrooms, no auditorium, no gymnasium, and, because of lack of staff, almost no outside recreation. The only assembly room is a small chapel. Men sit endlessly in their small double occupancy cells or in the crowded dormitories, and their bitterness and despair mounts. While we were there, one man sliced his wrists twice and was near death. We were surprised by the calmness with which inmate orderlies and female nurses handled the emergency until we were told by a high staff person that similar incidents occur on the average of three times a week.

In the nearby state of Georgia, another new reception and classification center contains vastly improved, though still limited, recreational facilities. It provides several courtyards in which a variety of physical activities is regularly scheduled. This institution at Jackson also offers a large and regularly used athletic field. Men however still spend most of their classification period behind the grilles of their inside cells.

But in a third southern state, Florida, the reception and classification center at Lake Butler is a veritable beehive of recreational activity. This center serves an identical purpose to its sister reception centers in nearby states; but, in contrast to their telephone pole, maximum security design, it is a campus-type facility. The several buildings are spread out over 52 acres which are enclosed by a double cyclone fence.

Florida, of course, has milder winters than most of the United States. On the days of our February visit the temperature hovered between 60 and 75 degrees. On those days, almost the entire reception population was scattered across the several acres playing volleyball, checkers, softball, basketball, football, lifting weights, or just sunning themselves. There is also a very large gymnasium big enough for two simultaneous basketball games. The gym also provides balconies for boxing and weight lifting and serves as auditorium and movie theater.

The contrast in inmate attitude and morale at these three institutions was most apparent to the members of our visiting team. Facilities for recreation, we concluded, cannot be viewed as luxuries. They are most essential. A warden explained the absence of a gymnasium at his institution. "Some high schools in this state," he said, "do not have gymnasiums." That is regrettable. High schools should have gyms, but the comparison ends there. The high school boy or girl spends six hours a day in the school building. He or she is actively and constructively occupied during most of that period and has available those Y's, parks, playgrounds, pools, lakes, theaters, mountains, and seashores that are available to free people. The prisoner, on the other hand, confined 24 hours a day for months and years on end can use only those facilities provided within the perimeter of the prison.

The administrators and architects who have planned most of America's newest correctional institutions have recognized the vital importance of ample recreational space and have tried within budgetary limitations to provide adequately. At the maximum security prison at Somers, Connecticut, for example, there are two large gymnasiums, side by side. Each of these, in addition to the basketball courts and weight lifting equipment, has three handball courts. One of these gymnasiums is also used as an auditorium. It has a stage and a booth for movie projection. Unique to Somers, at least as far as our travels took us, is a large television theater. It seats 500 to 700 persons. The television picture is projected onto a large movie-size screen. Television is a prime recreational activity — perhaps I should say nonactivity — in all institutions. Dayroom after dayroom has been surrendered to the tube. In several correctional centers, including Somers, an inmate who can afford to purchase a television set may have it in his cell. Strangely, to be allowed a television set in one's cell was an amenity available only to the men on death row at one prison that we visited.

The federal penitentiary at Marion has a wider variety of recreational activities available to its inmates than any other institution on our itinerary. Marion has gone through an evolutionary process. It was designed originally as a replacement for Alcatraz to hold the federal system's most intractable felons. The original design provided practically no activity and no dayrooms. Prisoners would be confined 20 of each 24 hours. Before it was opened, however, its function was changed. Rather than an institution for the intractables, it was to be a correctional center for younger offenders. As a result, provisions for extremely varied activity, especially recreational, were added. Consequently, Marion, which is now no longer used for youthful offenders, provides facilities for such disparate activities as tennis, lawn bowls, bocci, miniature golf, handball, track, and all

the team sports. We have never seen such ample provisions for weight lifting which, by the way, is a most popular activity in correctional institutions. Marion, however, still does not have dayrooms though it does have some television viewing areas.

We saw no swimming pools in institutions designed primarily for adult male felons. We did see pools in several youth and juvenile centers. The Michigan Training Unit at Ionia, for example, has an Olympic size pool. At Ionia there is an 11-acre compound built expressly for recreation. Within it, in addition to the pool, are tennis, handball, and basketball courts as well as baseball, soccer, football, and softball fields. The girls' institution at Macon, Georgia, has a superior pool with adjoining patio for picnics and cookouts. The Kennedy Center also has superb play fields, a winding stream, and a lake as well as a fine physical education building with a swimming pool. Morgantown also provides very ample dayrooms in which dances are regular events. Girls come for these dances from the University of West Virginia, the town of Morgantown, and the nearby Youth Development Center at Waynesburg, Pennsylvania.

The newer juvenile institutions are often magnificently endowed with recreational space. Most have gymnasiums equal to those in our best public schools. We saw pools, often handsome ones, at Gatesville in Texas, Skillman in New Jersey, Brookwood and Tryon in New York, and Loysville in Pennsylvania. The last named warrants a special note. Loysville is an old and largely obsolete physical plant on a lovely rolling campus in very rural and white Pennsylvania. The town is tiny and has exceedingly few recreational facilities. The institution possesses the region's only swimming pool. The superintendent, early in his administration, opened the pool to the townspeople. Now, a visitor to Loysville is astounded to see little 3-year-old white country girls playing gleefully with huge black lads from far away Philadelphia. The pool has been a vital bridge between the community and the training school.

At the brand new boys' school at Giddings, Texas, we saw an innovation. A large artificial lake has been dug out of the flat countryside. It is complete with an island and campsites, and a suspension bridge connects the island with the mainland. Boats are available and the lake is stocked with fish. The director's rationale behind all this is interesting. Texas, he observes, is full of streams and open places which city kids don't know how to use. He reasons that once children have learned to use the great Texas out-of-doors they will never again want to idle around urban street corners. There is a lot of the Jeffersonian in the Texas Youth Council operating philosophy.

In a similar vein it was refreshing to see the young lads and lasses at The Weeks School in Vermont canoeing together in the stream adjacent to that remarkable New England coeducation center for delinquent youngsters. The dedicated "Mr. Chips" who has run the place for a quarter of a century says no one has gotten pregnant yet. He impressed us as a man you can believe.

Most of the recreational facilities that we have described serve physically active people. All inmates are not athletes. Some are old, others just aren't cut out for vigorous activity, and still others are lovers of the quiet activities. Most institutions don't provide adequately for such interests. The day-rooms largely have been surrendered to television or ping-pong. Quiet corners for pairs to play dominoes, checkers, or chess don't exist. Most institutional managers rigorously enforce rules against "two in a room" because homosexuality is such an overwhelming preoccupation. We seldom saw little alcoves or small rooms for quiet activities, conversation, or classical music. Only in rare places such as Vienna, Fox Lake, and Purdy are there places where persons can practice musical instruments without disturbing everyone around.

I would be remiss if I didn't mention one youth center that, in my opinion, had an excellent recreational program in spite of a dearth of expensive facilities. The Arizona Youth Center near Tucson, Arizona, is blessed with extraordinarily good weather which permits outdoor activity almost around the calendar. The institution, therefore, does not have a gymnasium. There are, however, several black-top basketball courts and space for other team activities. The director is an unreformed "jock," yet one sees no intermural or interscholastic sports at Tucson. He insists that too many recreational programs are run for the few who are gifted athletes while all the rest remain unskilled thus retaining their sense of inadequacy. At Tucson we saw a lot of activity built around learning to play the game. The objective there is to get the boys comfortable enough about athletics so that they won't shrink away when sides are being chosen back in their home neighborhoods. There is no pool at Tucson and the director told us he prefers not to have one. His boys use the community pool as they will have to do when they return home.

In fact, we saw some new community correctional centers which purposely have almost no built-in recreational facilities. Among them are the several community treatment centers in Vermont, South Carolina, Florida, and Oregon. These centers are largely used for prerelease programs in which the inmates work and/or attend school in the community. The facility itself provides only essential services such as room and board. Church, school, medical care, work, and recreation are all provided by the same community resources that serve the general population. Nothing, during our long tour, impressed us more. They seemed to provide such reasonable and normal paths of reintegration to the community. We will discuss them in greater detail later.

Visiting

Staff and inmates alike spoke to us of the importance of visiting. It is usually the principal remnant of any direct, personal relationship with the outside world. The old policies based on maximum separation of the inmate from the influences of the outside world have been discredited. Today most correctional officials recognize that outside contacts are not only desirable but necessary. Offenders are humans, and humans are social beings.

The quality of the visiting experience varies enormously and is influenced by several factors. Fundamental, of course, is the defined purpose of the institution. Facilities designed to confine the most desperate offenders usually provide more rigid and less pleasant accommodations for the visitor. But this tendency is not absolute. We saw pleasant visiting facilities in very secure prisons such as the federal penitentiary at Marion, Illinois, and we saw unpleasant facilities in less secure and highly program-conscious institutions such as the youth center at Morganton, North Carolina. The situation there is a result of a change in the facility's function that developed between the design stage and the actual opening of the center.

Visiting arrangements which we observed fell into the following six categories:

(1) Closed Visit. The closed visit provides no opportunity for contact between the inmate and the visitors. A dividing partition extends from floor to ceiling forming a complete physical barrier between the prisoner and his or her loved ones. Usually a counter of table height extends along either side of the partition. Stools or chairs, often fastened to the floor, are provided, though we did observe at least four visiting rooms where prisoner and visitor had to stand.

Panels of glass or stainless steel mesh are built into the partitions to permit visual but not physical contact. When glass panels are utilized, either a small metal aperture or pairs of telephones are provided to allow the transmission of sound. Through the aperture, the voice is barely audible

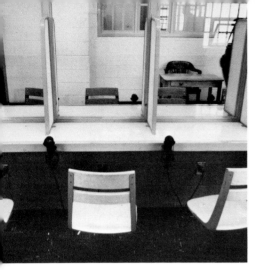

especially when the visiting room is crowded. The telephone is equally unsatisfactory as it provides distorted and depersonalized communication.

Closed visits are very easy to supervise because no physical contact can occur. Moreover, the phone arrangements permit monitoring of conversations and provide an impersonal method for terminating visits. The guard can merely disconnect the phone at the end of the stipulated period. In one instance the termination was automatic. And most important, from the security point of view, closed visits permit no passage of contraband—money, narcotics, or weapons. Prison officials are ever aware of the dangers inherent in the passage of contraband. They are quick to point out that the weapons George Jackson and Walter Elliott are alleged to have used recently to kill guards at San Quentin, California, and Norfolk, Massachusetts, could not have been brought into the prison during closed visits.

But for the typical offender—in fact the overwhelming majority of all offenders—the closed visit is unnecessary, unpleasant, and destructive to relationships with family, friends, and especially children. The impersonal quality of the closed visit is captured in Conrad Weiser's poem "Prison Green and Glass Partitions" part of which reads:

> *"We go to see him Sunday afternoons in the big dirty room with green walls and a glass between.*
>
> *Shoulder to shoulder with others who come on Sunday afternoon, nameless people shouting intimacies reserved for the quiet of a home."*

(2) Limited Contact Visit. This type of visit eliminates the dividing partition of the closed visit and substitutes a long table usually with a center partition extending from the floor to a few inches above the surface of the table. The purpose of the division is to impede the passage of contraband. Thus the visitor and the visited share the same room, speak without the impediments of phones or apertures, and usually are permitted greeting and departing handshakes and perhaps kisses. There can be close supervision by an officer who is frequently located at the head of the table.

This type of visiting facility is usually found in very secure institutions which are, nevertheless, willing to make the break from the total control and depersonalization inherent in the closed visit. A high degree of security is retained, but

under conditions more personal and satisfactory to both inmate and visitor. However, some by-products of the limited contact visit are unpleasant and degrading. The shoulder-to-shoulder congestion plus the ever-present close supervision of the officer keep intimacy and privacy to a minimum. Even more humiliating is the accompanying body search. The inmate enters the visiting room via a vestibule in which he may be searched to insure no outward passage of contraband. He may be required to change his clothes for a set that has been searched beforehand to insure that he carries no contraband into the visiting room. On completion of visiting, the process is reversed and intensified by visual inspection of the oral and anal cavities, and with women, we suppose, of the vagina. The visitor is also subject to security checks which frequently include passing through electronic detecting devices and the placing of handbags in locked boxes outside the visiting area.

(3) Informal Contact Visit. Our team saw many visiting facilities that provide for informal contact visiting. Strangely enough, we found them in institutions of all degrees of security, serving all types of offenders of both sexes and all ages—adult, youth, and juvenile. Visiting rooms that provide for the informal contact visit are usually furnished with comfortable chairs, small tables, davenports, and, sometimes, machines dispensing foods, sweets, and beverages. The furniture is often arranged so that visitors may sit together in natural and private groupings. Unfortunately, however, this is not always so. Some administrations have arranged the furniture rigidly so as to perpetuate the untrusting, formal, and impersonal atmosphere.

Several correctional authorities have, in recent years, extended the informality of their visiting arrangements to include picnic and play areas, and thus they have increased the normalcy of the inmate's contact with his relatives, friends, and, especially, his children. We found attractive picnic and play areas provided in some old maximum security prisons such as the Graterford and Western penitentiaries in Pennsylvania where new leadership is making the most of obsolete facilities. Most of the juvenile facilities, many of the newer medium and minimum security adult facilities, and some of the maximum security institutions for adults now provide attractively landscaped open air visiting areas.

In the more security-conscious institutions which offer contact visits in informal settings, the privilege of such visits is frequently limited to selected and trusted inmates. Closed or limited contact visiting rooms are retained for the remainder of the population. Moreover, custodial practices already described including body searches and electronic detecting devices, are imposed on the inmate and his visitor. In more open facilities, including some for women and most of those for children, searches are occasional, less intimate, and selective.

(4) Freedom of the Grounds. A few reduced security institutions that we visited – such as forestry camps, satellites, prerelease centers, and juvenile training schools – allow inmates and their visitors to enjoy total or limited freedom of the grounds. Parent and child, husband and wife, brothers and sisters are thus afforded a relaxed privacy and a degree of responsible freedom that quite likely contribute to a sense of worth and trust usually lacking in the correctional process. The vast majority, including the most open of the campus-type correctional centers, did not, however, permit such freedom during visits. The officials to whom we addressed the question, "Why not here?" feared that contraband, especially drugs and alcohol, would be the result. But by far their greatest concern was that sexual activity might result. The modern correctional official likes to use the cliché, "Men are sent here not for punishment, but as punishment." The denial to a man or a woman of normal sexual activity is viewed by many prison administrators as a fundamental purpose of imprisonment – society's ultimate punishment.

(5) Conjugal or Family Visit. If sexual repression was the hallmark of the Victorian period, then the correctional center must be the most Victorian of all American institutions. And because the free world of the young is no longer Victorian, the correctional institution, occupied predominantly by the young, is more irrelevant and repressive than ever. Correctional managers are committed to preventing heterosexual relationships between the inmate and his mate. At the same time, they expend much ingenuity and energy to repress homosexuality which is a product of the unisexual nature of most correctional institutions. Male wardens refuse to hire women out of fear that the male inmate will be excited to sexual activity by their presence. The woman superintendent, under a similar misapprehension, finds excuse after excuse not to employ male staff. These are admissions that the institution is not directed at, or related to, normal social life.

Two of the most rigid institutions that we visited were women's prisons which were run by almost exclusively female staffs. Concern with homosexuality seemed to be the overwhelming preoccupation of these staffs, and, as a result, suspicion, oversupervision, and consequent hostility were rampant. In two other equally small women's prisons, we found a mixed staff—male and female—and minimal preoccupation with homosexuality on the part of either the inmates or the employees.

We visited still another institution, a center for youth, at 9:30 one evening and found the entire student body in the gymnasium partaking of the most strenuous of calisthenics. I asked the official who was accompanying me about the significance of this. He replied, "We like to tire them out before they go to bed. Then they don't have so much energy for masturbation and homosexuality."

Probably the most "normal" institutions that we visited were coeducational training schools in Vermont and Washington where boys and girls associated freely and normally with each other, as young people do in communities and schools all over America. Coeducation in corrections is spreading, and recently (but after our visit) the Robert F. Kennedy Youth Center in Morgantown, West Virginia, became coeducational. The new 16-story correctional center in Morganton, North Carolina, will shortly, we were told by its superintendent, receive both male and female offenders. But because of the design of this multistory building, the sexes will be almost completely segregated.

In spite of the manifold problems which unisexuality creates for correctional administrators, only one of the more than 100 new institutions which we visited permitted conjugal visits on institutional grounds. The basic reason, of course, is fear of public disapproval. Officials, who admit that they have miles to go before their institutions qualify for the euphemism "correctional" fear that the public outcry against allowing heterosexual practices in prisons would delay progress in less controversial areas. Apparently the occasional public outcry against homosexual activity is less threatening. Moreover, the inevitable questions arise: Who would be permitted? Married persons? Persons who have lived in common law? Lovers who had known a substantial and continuing relationship? Transient lovers? Prostitutes? And even if those questions were answered, how would the institution be protected against contraband, pregnancies, venereal disease, and inmate jealousies?

the "red houses" at Parchman

Most correctional administrators have decided that all these are policy questions that are either not worth answering or should be answered negatively. They are fortified by the reality that their correctional facilities have not been designed to allow heterosexual intercourse with safety and in dignity. Where would they permit it? In the cells? In a special unit? In a little red house in a remote part of the prison grounds? In any case, to escort a man and a woman to a specially designed room for a brief period of sexual intercourse dehumanizes the whole relationship.

We visited several new facilities that are built in such a way that conjugal visits could be a dignified and normal experience. A motel-like prerelease center in Maryland, the honor cottages at the Kennedy Center in West Virginia, the "outmate" apartments of the Purdy Treatment Center for Women in Washington, and the Illinois State Penitentiary at Vienna all are nearly ready, from an architectural point of view, and await only public approval and the administrators' decision to bring heterosexual activity into the correctional experience.

Two states have already officially taken the natural, but bold step. Mississippi, as long as can be remembered, has permitted conjugal visits at its prison farm at Parchman.

Parchman is in reality a huge plantation of over 21,000 acres. Hence the buildings and other facilities differ from most prisons. They are spread out over several miles with small work camps dotted throughout the vast expanse. Central to these camps are housing wings of open dormitories much like a military barracks. Wire fences surround a few of these barracks but most are quite open.

Because we did not visit Parchman, we have borrowed from the penitentiary's booklet describing visits. It was written by Columbus B. Hopper, an associate professor of sociology at the University of Mississippi. We think it interesting enough to repeat in considerable detail.

> . . . *Parchman apparently has the most liberal visitation program of any state penitentiary in the United States. The institution not only emphasizes bringing visitors into the prison, but also allows the inmates to keep in contact with their families by leaving the prison themselves. . . . Under the existing leave program at Parchman, called the 'Holiday Suspension Program,' each year from December 1 until March 1, selected inmates who have been at the penitentiary at least 3 years with good behavior records may go home for a period of 10 days. . . .*
>
> *All visiting by the inmates' families occurs on Sunday afternoons; inmates may receive visits from their families each Sunday. . . . They come mostly in private automobiles, although some may come by bus and taxi. Visiting hours are from 1 o'clock until 5 o'clock. The third Sunday is called 'Big Sunday' because of the longer visiting hours. . . .*
>
> *While waiting for the visiting hours to start, the visitors*

wait in their cars parked on the side of the highway in front of the administration building. As the visiting hours draw near, they drive to the main entrance and clear themselves with a guard. After a brief inspection of the car, consisting usually of the guard's looking into the car and recording the license plate, the visitors drive by the administration building, past the hospital, and out on the plantation to the camp that houses the inmates they wish to visit.

On arrival at the camp the visitors must undergo another inspection by the camp sergeant or the guard on duty at the entrance of the camp grounds. This inspection is more rigid than the inspection at the main entrance, particularly if it is the first time a visitor has appeared at the camp. The visitors must identify themselves, and if requested, submit to being searched. The guard looks into the car trunk and records the visitors' names. . . . The inmate then is allowed to come out of the camp building unguarded, receive his visitors and visit with them anywhere within the camp area.

The grounds around each camp building are extensive enough to allow inmates and their visitors room enough to be by themselves, considerably removed from any other inmates or staff members. The penitentiary provides tables and benches for inmates and their visitors. When the weather is warm, the grounds around a camp building, although less crowded, look somewhat like a city park on a Sunday afternoon. People sit on blankets eating picnic lunches; others sit on benches in the shade of trees, while others walk around. Viewers may even see a boy and his father having a game of catch with a baseball, or children playing by themselves on swings or slides.

. . . For the married male inmate, the visiting freedom means that he may see his wife in private. And he may go with her into a private room, all alone, in a little building on the camp grounds and have coitus. . . . The conjugal visit is considered to be a part of the family visitation and home visitation programs. The family visit is emphasized at Parchman, and the conjugal visit is believed to be a logical part of the visiting program. . . .

The buildings used for the conjugal visits are referred to by the inmates and staff as "red houses." No employees at Parchman remembered the origin of this term. Apparently the first building provided for the visits was red in color, and inmates talking about it spoke of it as the red building or house. Most of the existing red houses are simple frame buildings with about five or six rooms, although some have as many as ten. The rooms are small and sparsely furnished; in each there is only a bed, a table and in some a mirror. A bathroom which the wives may use is located in each building.

Mississippi does not discriminate. Last year it authorized conjugal visits for women prisoners.

In 1968 California initiated a program of Family Visiting at its correctional facility at Tehachapi. This has subsequently spread to the state's other prisons. In California the emphasis has not been primarily on the sexual aspects of this program. Rather the program attempts to provide opportunity for entire families to visit together in privacy. The department's emphasis has been on sustaining family life as a bulwark against the breakup of marriages. Attractively furnished cottages, many of them formerly staff residences, mobile homes, and small buildings converted for other uses have been acquired for this expressed purpose. California authorities tell us that about half of the state's nearly 20,000 inmates are now eligible for family visits and 4,000 such visits are expected this year.

We observed the facilities at Chino and were impressed by them. But more importantly we were convinced that California's approach to allowing men and their legal wives to be alone together was not only mature, but civilized.

(6) Furloughs. Though this is a book about correctional facilities, we would be remiss if we didn't at least mention "furloughs" as a visiting option because, as is often the case, the best solution to a correctional problem is not a new facility but the existing resources of the community.

Furloughs have been part of the juvenile correctional scene for decades. One of my early recollections was a study I conducted in Minnesota nearly two decades ago. The superintendent of Red Wing, a juvenile training school, had become a legend in his time. One of the stories recounted about him concerned how a furlough policy of his won him undying devotion and support from the state's legislature. In those days the appropriation committee of the legislature visited each institution to review the budget requests. This superintendent, that December, was finding the committee less than receptive to his request for increased appropriation when a subordinate interrupted to whisper in his ear. Thereupon the superintendent rose, faced the committee and said, "Gentlemen, I am sorry, but important as you are to Red Wing I must leave you. Our staff has been able to arrange Christmas furloughs for every lad here except one. Right now that boy, not my budget, is my most important responsibility," and he left. I am told that he got every penny requested.

All the juvenile institutions that we visited had provisions for furloughs and day passes. Parents and relatives who visited were permitted to "sign out" their son or daughter to take to a movie, to go to dinner, or even to go home for the weekend. This practice has begun to spread, in a very limited way, to the adult correctional field. Its original use was limited to emergencies such as illness or death of a close relative. Later, prerelease and work release programs were started, and specialized facilities were created for those purposes. These have developed to an appreciable degree and we observed them in quite developed form in Vermont,

South Carolina, Oregon, Maryland, and Florida. Though they are prerelease centers, trusted inmates are often transferred to them reasonably early, and some spend up to two years in these community facilities. Generally these centers do not duplicate available community services such as recreation, church, work, social services, and education. The offender uses the same facilities and programs that the general public uses. Passes and furloughs are granted for a variety of legitimate purposes, including visiting one's family.

The furloughs have become a reasonable solution to the conjugal visit problems described above. Male and female inmates visit their spouses and sweethearts and do the tender and often intimate things that spouses and sweethearts have been doing since the beginning of time.

In summary, it seems reasonable to say that nearly all present facilities are lacking in the physical qualities which will allow private visiting even if it were wanted by the administrations. The humiliation of the nonperson is complete even in this "best" moment when inmate and loved ones are together. Only in California did we see an indoor place where a family could gather privately.

Program

When the pioneer penitentiaries were being planned and constructed, early in the 19th century, practitioners and theorists held three factors to be the primary contributors to criminal behavior. The first was environment. Report after report on offenders pointed out the harmful effects of family, home, and other aspects of environment on the offender's behavior. The second factor usually cited was the offender's lack of intelligence, aptitude, and work skills which led to indolence and a life of crime. The third cause was seen as the felon's ignorance of right and wrong because he had not been taught the Scriptures.

The social planners of the first quarter of the 19th century designed prison architecture and program to create an experience for the offender in which (1) there would be no injurious outside influences; (2) the offender would learn the value of labor and work skills; and (3) he would have the opportunity to learn about the Scriptures and accept from them the principles of right and wrong that should then guide his life.

The various states pursued this triad of purposes by one of two basic methods. The Pennsylvania System was based on solitary confinement, accompanied by bench labor within one's cell. There the offender was denied all contact with the outside world except that provided by the Scriptures, religious tracts, and visits from specially selected, exemplary citizens. The prison was designed painstakingly to make this kind of solitary experience possible. The walls between cells were thick and the cells themselves were large, each equipped with plumbing and hot water heat. In the cell were a workbench and tools. In addition, each cell had its own small walled area for solitary recreation. The institution was designed magnificently for its three purposes; elimination of external influences; provision of work; and opportunity for penitence, introspection, and acquisition of religious knowledge.

New York's Auburn System pursued the same three goals, but by a different method. Like the Pennsylvania System, it isolated the offender from the world outside permitting him virtually no external contact. However, it provided small cells in which the convicts were confined on the Sabbath and during nonworking hours. During working hours inmates labored in factory-like shops. The contaminating effect of the congregate work situation was to be eliminated by a rule of silence. Inmates were prohibited from communicating in any way with other inmates or the jailers.

The relative merits of these two systems were debated vigorously for half a century. The Auburn System ultimately prevailed in the United States, because it was less expensive and lent itself more easily to the production methods of the industrial revolution.

Both systems were disappointments almost from the beginning. The awful solitude of the Pennsylvania System reportedly drove men insane. The rule of silence of the Auburn System became increasingly unenforceable despite regular use of the lash, solitary confinement, and a variety of other harsh and brutal devices for punishment.

Imprisonment as an instrument of reform was an early failure. In the two centuries of the history of corrections one treatment concept after another has been evolved and absorbed into the system in continuous efforts to overcome the inherent weaknesses of confinement. Thus, to the original correctional treatment methods—isolation, work, and penitence—were added recreation, classification, vocational training, academic education, education for living, individual psychotherapy, pastoral counseling, medicine, psychopharmacological approaches, social casework, group therapy, milieu therapy, behavior modification, confrontation groups, transactional analysis, and community involvement. Still others are being added.

We saw many of these, in various combinations, in the institutions which we visited. Because most of these make demands upon the physical resources of the correctional centers, we will discuss them briefly. In doing so, it is not our intent to make a thorough analysis or evaluation of the various approaches or methodologies which we observed. Rather we will describe them in the context in which we saw them without trying to compare or evaluate the relative values of their approaches.

Regardless of the availability or inavailability of other programs, work, most often liberally mixed with idleness, was part of the regimen in every institution for adults that we visited. The nature of the work can be categorized as follows: **Work**

(1) *Cadre-type jobs.* Every institution employs inmates to perform many of the tasks necessary to its operation. These include janitoring, plant maintenance, dog robbing,* food preparation and service, clerical and stenography, water treatment, sewage disposal, power plant operation, landscaping, teaching, medical services, and in some rare instances — guarding. Anywhere between one- and two-thirds of the population of typical correctional institutions for male adults work at employment of this type. Most often we found two, three, and even more persons assigned to a task that would, on the outside, employ one. This seemed to be especially true of unskilled jobs for men carrying a maximum or medium security classification. Apparently our prisons hold large numbers of low skilled persons who, in the eyes of their keepers, are neither trainable nor trustworthy. Many of these people spend their sentences assigned to very part-time and, at least to them, meaningless work. They are, to use Willie Sutton's words, "confined within a vacuum of idleness for which they are paid a paltry few cents a day while whatever mental apparatus they might have deteriorates."

All cadre jobs are not meaningless. In fact some of them are very vital to prison operations. The captain's clerk, for example, is a highly trained technician exercising enormous personal power. But he is employed at a job which has no free world counterpart. A great deal of prison employment constitutes "trained incapacity."

(2) *Road, Farm, and Forest.* Scattered around rural America are hundreds of institutions, mostly small, which have been created to provide labor to build and maintain roads, operate farms, and care for our streams and forests. Most, but not all, of these institutions are categorized as minimum security. They are relatively open, and consequently custody is a function of classification rather than of prison hardware. The principal exceptions to the above are the huge prison plantations on which entire penal populations serve time. We did not visit any "plantation-type" prisons.

Most camp-type facilities have been created to serve the economic needs of society and only incidentally the correctional needs of the offenders. Cotton is picked, lumber is cut, livestock is raised, crops are harvested, roads are built, forest fires are fought, and parks and state buildings are maintained. These are all legitimate tasks for prisoners, especially while our system still (1) receives large numbers of offenders who are a minimal threat to themselves and to the general public, and (2) holds men long after they are

*Dog robber is military parlance for flunky, orderly, errand boy.

ready for freedom. Moreover, open facilities do serve therapeutic purposes by removing men from the stifling prison environment, separating the young and unsophisticated from the predators, and substituting controls based upon trust rather than bars. All these aspects are laudable.

However, important deficiencies exist. These remote facilities seldom provide educational or service resources. The predominantly rural-type labor usually bears no relationship to the work skills required by urban offenders. Moreover, separation of the prisoner from his real world is almost as complete as it would have been in the penitentiary. Visits are difficult to arrange because of distances from hometowns.

The future of these remote camps is subject to conjecture especially if restless city blacks should begin to escape into rural white America, and if community correctional programs should cause many of the more stable and less dangerous offenders to be siphoned out of the state's prison system. As society finds still more noninstitutional community-based solutions to its problems, the rural open institutions will become harder and harder to populate and will become white elephants. Already they are operating farther below their rated capacities than any other type of correctional facility.

We saw several correctional centers of medium and even maximum security classification that operate large farms or forestry services outside their security perimeters. The Sierra Conservation Center in California is an example. This is a large (1,200 capacity) medium security facility at the foothills of the Sierras. It was designed to receive selected inmates destined in time to work in one or another of the center's many small forestry satellites located throughout the California mountains. All housing at the center is in open dormitories, the size of which was predetermined by the size of the work gangs. The prime program at Sierra is training for forestry work and the major industrial activity is related to the conservation function. Other activities, such as education and counseling, are seldom available.

We visited one of the center's many satellites. It is not unlike a small military or civilian conservation camp of the 1930's and '40's. The buildings are of temporary construction, the dormitories are open, and inside recreation is limited. The work is physical—building fire breaks, clearing out underbrush, planting, clearing streams, and fighting forest fires. The setting is spectacularly beautiful, and the morale quite high. The chief complaints of the men were about the camp's distance from the population centers from which they came, the lack of programs, the exploitative nature of the work, and the camp's failure to prepare them for available outside employment.

At Sierra we saw an erosion that will, as we have already observed, eventually reach most reduced custody correc-

*A combination
of maintenance,
industrial,
and agricultural
activities
constitutes
prison work.*

tional centers. The California probation subsidy program is diverting the less dangerous offenders from the state penal system. The maximum security population is holding, but the minimum security population is diminishing. As a result, many of the satellites are being forced to close. Even the Sierra Conservation Center itself is undergoing a population shift. The new more difficult inmate population requires more security than has been built into Sierra. It especially requires individual rooms rather than open dormitories, more facilities for counseling and vocational education, and more industry within the security perimeter. This is but one of many examples of a facility that was originally designed for a specific program and type of inmate. The rapidly changing nature of corrections has already rendered Sierra inappropriate for its present and future uses.

Much of the entire Colorado prison population is at Canon City where the reception center, the maximum security penitentiary, the women's prison, and the medium security penitentiary are all located within a five mile radius of one another. The medium security facility provides a vocational program including body and automobile repair, welding, a machine shop, and a laundry, but its chief industry is its agricultural complex. The farm includes a large truck garden, a dairy, a beef herd, and a most remarkable germ-proof piggery (where I spent a fascinating two hours).

On the day of our visit the maximum security prison was nearly at capacity, the reformatory was above capacity, but the medium security institution was at less than half of capacity. Only 275 men were occupying the relatively new 600-bed facility. Apparently Colorado, like other states, is finding it difficult to fill its reduced custody institutions.

The medium security prison at Carson City, Nevada, is a new correctional institution that not only works its inmates on outlying farms but also on the grounds of the state capital. The staff at Carson City, like those at other similar institutions, would prefer not to have to move large numbers of inmates in and out through the security perimeter each day. The opportunity for introduction of contraband is great. The result is the unpleasant (to both staff and inmate) necessity of body-frisking men who were in trusted details all day. The administration would prefer the creation of a small camp outside the security perimeter for those men. It is noted that the federal penitentiary at Marion, Illinois, in mid-1972, built such a camp outside the walls for its minimum custody workers.

(3) *Prison Industries*. In the old days, according to prison historians, penitentiaries were busy places. Wardens worked their prisoners at contract labor, competed with private industry and free labor, and ran pretty terrible road gangs, farms, and sweatshops. In the late 1920's and early '30's, the labor movement pressed for federal and state laws to eliminate the competition of prison labor and other conditions. The result has been a "state use" system of

prison industry that has contributed greatly to the idleness described earlier. Under this system only public agencies may use or buy prison-made products. The system is designed to avoid direct competition with free enterprise and labor. It often is inefficient, with little modern machinery, and is overstaffed with inmate workers who produce inferior goods at excessive costs. The result has often been that only a few inmates have productive work while others are either completely idle or engaged in make-believe tasks. Such policies, rather than helping a person toward self-sufficiency, lead him to abject dependency, poor work habits, and, quite likely, recidivism.

Probably the worst instance of inadequate industry that we observed was at the Holman maximum security unit. On the days of our visit to that benighted place we found most of its 800 men in total or near idleness. A cadre detail of 150 performed tasks that could efficiently be handled by one-third that number. Over 100 others were assigned to the prison's only industry, a license plate factory. The actual work there was performed by about 20 men. We also observed two details of men refusing to rake the frozen January earth. They were under the eyes of armed and mounted guards. Though there was no meaningful purpose to their task the warden did persuade them that it was to their benefit to rake. They returned to their useless activity only because the inhuman segregation unit was an even more dismal alternative.

Near Charleston, South Carolina, we visited a correctional institution that was built around just one industry — the largest laundry in the southeastern part of the United States. This massive laundry serves not only the penal institutions, but the mental health facilities, and the University of South Carolina. Since its opening in 1963, educational facilities and programs have been added, and now the institution is less single-purposed than it once was. It remains, however, a prison with but one, repetitive task — to wash dirty linens.

At a handsomely designed, newly opened medium security prison at Leesburg, New Jersey, an outstanding model of architectural planning, we saw much that was structurally exciting and innovative. But not so with the industrial program that we observed. It consisted of an automated tag shop that employed very few men constructively and a sewing shop in which shirts and other garments were made. Already, in this most attractive new institution, men were grumbling (at least to us) about the meaninglessness of their work experience. As one man put it, "This is the same old shit in a pretty setting."

We found the medium security center at Fox Lake, Wisconsin, and the maximum security prisons at Somers, Connecticut, and Marion, Illinois, to have the most adequate industrial programs of any institutions on our itinerary. All have modern, large industrial buildings that are well-lighted and ventilated. The Fox Lake operation is essentially a furniture enterprise but because it makes such a wide range of products, the industry provides for a variety of skills. The plant has wood furniture, tubular furniture, and upholstering divisions, and all were busy on the days of our visits.

Industrial activities at Somers include a large laundry, a furniture factory, upholstering and furniture refinishing shops, a data processing plant, a clothing factory, print and typewriter repair shops, and a well-equipped maintenance center. The federal penitentiary at Marion, like all other federal prisons, benefits from the fact that the huge federal civilian and military establishments are enormous markets for prison-made products. Thus idleness is less prevalent in the federal prison system. At Marion we saw a very large and complete printing industry, as well as a furniture factory that seemed to have an endless demand for its desks, tables, and other products. It is my recollection that only at Marion did we find air conditioning in an industrial building. We note, however, that even in the comparatively affluent federal system only 5,700 of its 22,000 prisoners are employed in prison industries. That's only 26%. We also felt, at Marion, a tightness and hostility in the atmosphere which was foreboding.

Industrial activity has been largely neglected in the institutions for women that we visited. Canon City, Colorado, for example, has only a small sewing room, a laundry, and, as in all women's prisons, a beauty shop. The women's prison at Carson City, Nevada, has practically no industry — only cadre-type activities such as food service, sanitary activities, and the ever-present beauty shop. A few women work at the governor's mansion a few miles away. Salem, Oregon, has small ironing and sewing rooms, the inevitable beauty shop, and the usual service activities. Even the extraordinary new women's institution in Washington provides only limited constructive work—a small data processing activity, and again the sewing room and beauty shop. Women, like men, serve lengthy sentences and require more than educational and treatment activities. Meaningful work is important not only to their well-being while incarcerated, but to their future employability.

Prison labor in America is slave labor. The prisoner works for his board, as a diversion from total boredom, and for a miserable few pennies a day. As a result his incentive is nil, his productivity low, and his commitment to any work ethic eroded. American corrections, we are convinced, must join the marketplace, pay its workers accordingly, charge them for many of the expenses of their keep, permit them to support their families, and require them to pay indemnities to their victims. Some of the work release programs have set the stage for such developments.

(4) *Work Release Programs.* The first work release law was passed several decades ago in Wisconsin, but this method of

employing inmates from state prisons has only just begun to gain momentum. We observed excellent work release programs for women offenders in both Oregon and Washington, and for male offenders in many states. Noteworthy among these are Vermont, South Carolina, Maryland, Wisconsin, North Carolina, and Oregon. Work release is a step in the direction of community corrections in that the offender, while serving an institutional sentence, works at a real job in the real world.

South Carolina provides a good example of how work release operates. An inmate in that state becomes eligible for the program one year prior to release. He may then be transferred from one of the state's prisons to the prerelease center nearest his home. There, often with his own participation, he is found a job where he is paid the prevailing wages. From his earnings he must pay room and board ($3.50/day) and also save a minimum of $5.00/week. From the amount remaining he may make an allotment to his family, pay union dues, and purchase clothes or special items such as radios and electric razors. He is allowed to retain $10.00 each week to pay the miscellaneous expenses made necessary by his status as a working man. While on work release status he is permitted no drugs or liquor, may not visit bars, and is limited in his movements and associations. He must be back at the prerelease center each night.

By the time of our visit to prerelease centers in South Carolina, the inmates in the program had paid $134,000 in taxes and $281,000 to the department for room and board. They had disbursed $210,000 to their dependents; spent $218,000 on clothes, amenities, and pocket money; and saved $357,000 for use on their release. Persons released from this program took home with them nest eggs averaging close to $1,000. This fact alone may be a major cause of a substantial reduction in South Carolina's recidivism rate for those participating in the program. The more meaningful work experience may be a second reason.

(5) *Contracts with Private Industry.* This nation has always had a commitment to private enterprise. With regard to prison industry this commitment ended with the passage of "state use" laws. The earlier exploitation of prison labor by private entrepreneurs working with prison officials was a major reason why those laws were found to be necessary. An unfortunate by-product has been a prison industry that is largely inefficient, which uses antiquated methods, which keeps large numbers of prisoners in total or substantial idleness, and which, because of the methods and pay scale it employs, fails to encourage or reward initiative.

Many correctional leaders are thinking that the time has come to use once again the strength and vitality of the private enterprise system. These leaders argue that organized labor and business interests are no longer passionately concerned about prison-made products competing in the free market. There is even evidence, they say, that free labor and industry are willing to join with prison officials to plan and update prison industries even to the extent of running them under contract. The partnership between labor, private enterprise, and the prison establishments would insure more efficient and relevant industries, providing work experiences related to the kind of work offenders will do after release.

This of course would necessitate paying the prisoner prevailing wages. It would probably demand his unionization. It would also require the modernizing of the prison shops. Prisoners, like those on work release in South Carolina, would be required to pay room and board, support their dependents, and save toward their release.

Though we heard this model for prison industry freely discussed as we traveled the country, we did not see any prison in which the ideas were being implemented.

Vocational Training

The correctional population is overwhelmingly a young and unskilled population. It would seem, therefore, that a primary program priority should be the provision of meaningful vocational training. It is indeed a priority at many of the new institutions that we visited, and the physical resources made available for vocational training are frequently impressive. Among the most admirable are new facilities at Ionia, Michigan; Fox Lake, Wisconsin; Shelton, Washington; Yardville, New Jersey; Morgantown, West Virginia; Hagerstown, Maryland; and the MacDougall Youth Center in South Carolina.

The Maryland Correctional Training Center at Hagerstown was designed by a former commissioner of that state who fervently believed that work was the most effective of all correctional programs. He had already built in Maryland one of the most extensive "state use" prison industries in the country. At the new training center he planned to train young and tractable offenders for skills usable in prison industries and on the outside. The new institution's central activity was to be vocational training and a carefully planned building was constructed for that purpose. It contains nine distinct shops, each complete with an adjacent classroom in which the theoretical aspects of vocational training are taught. Much of the theoretical instruction is of the self-teaching variety. Each student has a cubicle equipped with visual and audio aids. This permits the men to proceed at their own speed. It also allows the instructor to remain, most of the time, in the vocational shops where most of the action occurs. The trouble with Hagerstown vocational training is that it is just not large enough to be adequate. This is a big correctional center housing well over 1,000 offenders. Its facilities, other than housing, appear sufficient for only half that number. Hagerstown, like so many centers visited, suffers from too little program for too many inmates.

The Michigan Training Unit at Ionia is, it seems to me, a remarkable special purpose institution. In order for a person to be transferred to the training unit, he must be competent and capable of learning, and he must show motivation. If he proves incapable or unmotivated he does not remain. Perhaps this selection process contributes to the high morale and sense of purpose that seemed to pervade the place during the days of our visit.

This immaculately maintained institution concentrates on academic education and vocational training. The school building is very much like any good school on the outside, and it has an unusually fine library. The vocational education section contains shops providing instruction in welding, woodwork, automobile mechanics, body repair, barbering, drafting, refrigeration repair, air conditioning maintenance, data processing, and baking. As at Hagerstown, each vocational shop has an adjacent theory classroom. To me, and I have been in so many institutions that I am not too easily fooled, these looked like real learning shops, and all were extremely busy when I visited.

To digress, there are a lot of little things about Ionia which suggest that its planners and administrators respect the human beings who come to it and that its residents reciprocate that respect. The toilets are one example. They, unlike most toilets in men's institutions, are provided with modesty partitions. The dayrooms are another. Ionia is, I believe, the only institution that we visited that provides dayrooms for quiet activities such as checkers, bridge, chess, or just plain reading, as well as dayrooms for television and ping-pong. The reciprocation was apparent in the elegant care inmates took of the buildings and grounds.

The vocational training facilities and programs at Fox Lake in Wisconsin were, like so much of that institution, excellent. Here, as at Ionia, we felt that the effort at training young men was a most sincere one carried out by dedicated instructors in very adequate shops and classrooms. At Fox Lake, however, we were made aware of a racial situation that we were to see over and over again. The vocational teaching staff, like so much of all correctional staff, was white, while a substantial proportion of the students was black. Many of the white, often ethnic, tradesmen who teach vocational education in correctional institutions across the country fail to comprehend the negative attitudes of some blacks toward the craft training opportunities offered them in our better institutions. An instructor at Fox Lake, however, understood and made that understanding abundantly clear to me. Pointing to one black who had just built a fancy brick wall in a masonry class, he said, "Poor devil, he'll never in a million years get into a bricklayers' union in Wisconsin."

Many institutions have been conceived to serve one purpose, but, because of the exigencies of an ever-changing world, end up performing an entirely different function.

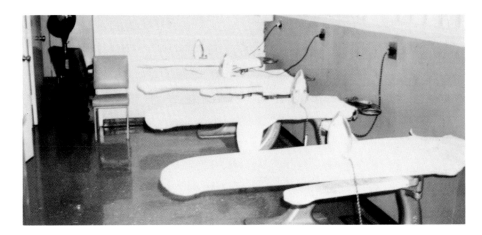

Bordentown in New Jersey, for example, was designed as a medium security farm for older and more stable offenders but was converted to serve a youthful, escape-prone, acting-out population. Marion, the federal penitentiary, has gone the cycle from maximum security prison to correctional center for youthful offenders back again to maximum security prison. Caught in this process of change, correctional officials learn to "make do." Morganton, a brand new correctional center for youthful offenders in western North Carolina is a case in point. We have mentioned this high-rise prison before and we shall again when we discuss behavior modification, but for now I want to discuss its vocational training program.

Morganton was first designed, we were told, after a riot at the old state prison at Raleigh. It was to serve as a maximum security prison for the western half of the state. Later, after construction was well along but before occupancy, its purpose was redefined to serve the state's youthful felons. Unfortunately, no vocational shops and only one substantial industry were built into the new prison. That industry was the operation of a huge commissary to prepare all the food for the many institutions in western North Carolina.

For its new, youthful population this was changed. No longer would Morganton prepare food for other institutions. Rather its kitchen, bakeries, and butcher shops would provide vocational training. In a very real way this is the institution's only resource for vocational education. Hopefully, college instructors will help Morganton become a center for training of gourmet chefs. We hope it works. This new institution has just opened under intelligent and enthusiastic leadership. To us, however, it appears that the architectural limitations of this unusual correctional center will cause it unimagined problems.

Education   The correctional education facilities and programs that we observed are mixed bags. Some facilities are cramped jerry-built arrangements and one-room schoolhouses, while others compare most favorably with school buildings in the free world. The programs range from glorified baby-sitting (sometimes for adults) to inspired efforts at compensatory education. The administration of some institutions, especially those for juveniles and youthful offenders, saw their primary role as that of educator, and they regarded their correctional institutions as residential schools for disadvantaged young people. And some were precisely that.

The Weeks School in Vermont is, of the facilities we visited, the one that seems most nearly to fill that description. This is not a new institution. In fact, it was opened in 1865. We had not, therefore, placed it on our itinerary. But because it was on our route between two other institutions we stopped in. It is beautifully located with buildings, old and new, scattered over several acres of magnificent New England campus. To the stranger passing by, it might be mistaken for an expensive boarding school except that it is coeducational. Most New England preparatory schools are not.

Our notes read, after the visit to Vermont started, "If there is such a thing as a good institution for young people, The Weeks School must be that institution." There were several factors that contributed to this conclusion. Its homogeneity eliminated some sources of conflict. The site is lovely. The houseparents and teachers seemed unusually competent. But fundamentally the reason was leadership. The superintendent of many years (who retired just after our visit) refused to see his school as a correctional institution. He insisted, regardless of the court commitments of his students, that Weeks is a school. He admitted that it is a school for youngsters with special problems, but added, "If they were richer they would go to private schools." He saw his job to be that of making Weeks every bit as good and its staff every bit as concerned as those of private schools.

The school building is the newest complex on campus and is quite attractive. However, it serves only the junior high age child. Those of high school age attend the two regional high schools—one academic and one vocational. The superintendent's office is covered with over 200 photographs of beautiful children in graduation clothes and pose. They are The Weeks School lads and lasses who have graduated from the local high schools. I asked him, "Why all those pictures?" Quickly he said, "Because I love them." Then he added that it's good for newly admitted children to see testimony of the successes of their predecessors. The teachers with whom we talked had caught their superintendent's ardor for the children and the objectives of the program.

I wish we had some statistics on recidivism at Weeks.

The Weeks School is in lush, verdant Vermont. In the desert outside of Tucson, Arizona, we found another institution with some of the same quality. It is called the Arizona Youth Center, and it is for 12- to 14-year-old delinquent boys, an age group too young, in our opinion, for institutionalization. As far as we could observe during our two days there, it offered primarily two major program thrusts— relationship and education. The education building is a low-lying one-story structure that fits into the desert landscape. It has no hallways, all rooms being entered from the outside. This is feasible in dry, warm Arizona. Most delinquent children are retarded educationally, and the emphasis at Tucson is on remedial instruction in an accepting milieu. Though the institution's operations are staffed almost exclusively by virile-looking athletes from nearby University of Arizona, the teachers in the education department are, with one exception, women. Most of them are young, and all with whom I talked loved their work.

Apparently the children respond. We talked to scores of the young people, most of whom had hated school in their communities where, they said, each mistake was ridiculed. A problem, it seemed, was that they find so much acceptance in the school program at the Arizona Youth Center that they fear to return home. The school has an unusual library full of paperback books. A professor at the University of Michigan, Dr. Daniel Fader, had developed a technique for improving reading and writing skills by use of inexpensive but exciting novels available in paperback. These books, one teacher told us, were the coin of the realm there. The kids traded for them. This seemed to us to be relevant education. So did a young music instructor's effort at teaching a folk song. It was an inspirational Simon and Garfunkel number about a boy in trouble.

We saw remarkable facilities for education at the correctional centers operated by the Texas Youth Council at Gatesville, Giddings, and Brownwood. Education is the core of the program of the Texas Youth Council whose director firmly believes that delinquent kids are the products of poor schools and poor environments. He rejects, therefore, the currently popular ideas about community-based corrections because that kind of correctional program ties the child to the very schools and environment that have failed him.

He has apparently convinced the Texas legislature of his philosophy, and it has provided him with the financial means to build quite expensive corrective facilities that contain magnificent school buildings. The one for girls at Brownwood is a prime example. Built around a center courtyard, its handsome classrooms and equipment surpass anything we have seen.

The educational program can perhaps be best described by quoting from the handbook provided each new girl.

> *In today's world a person's educational and vocational training may well be the key to a successful adjustment in the community. Each girl will be given an academic assessment to determine the grade level at which she is currently functioning.... Our school system is programmed to allow a concentrated effort toward the removal of deficiencies in educational development and free her emotional energy....*
>
> *...Classes are set up so that a child can receive more time and emphasis in areas of difficulty or deprivation. It will also capitalize on her areas of strength....*
>
> *She will also be introduced to several vocational areas in order to help her begin setting goals for her future vocational training....*
>
> *...There will be some specialized vocational courses offered that are designed to develop an immediate saleable skill upon completion....*
>
> *... The school's basic philosophy is one of resocialization and rehabilitation. Accomplishment of these basic goals ... can best be achieved through the use of the child's motivation and desire to succeed and master basic educational and vocational skills....*

Education has been America's attempted answer to many problems which are perhaps unanswerable. It is so in the correctional institutions—especially those for juveniles—that we visited. Most had excellent—if sometimes traditional—educational plants and programs. Most of these educational plants and programs are operated 11 rather than 9 months each year. Apparently the extra pay attracts and holds teachers. Classes that we observed were somewhat smaller than on the outside, but furniture, equipment, and room arrangement seemed to follow the traditional public school format. Exceptions were at Stockton, California, where walls between rooms had been removed to provide space for team teaching; Morgantown, West Virginia, where furniture was arranged in seminar fashion and where closed circuit television was being creatively employed; and Morganton, North Carolina, where the dayrooms of each housing unit doubled as classrooms. At Smyrna in Delaware we saw an adult educational program that made use of the headsets installed in each cell. At regular hours educational programs, prepared at a nearby college, were piped into individual rooms via selected channels.

It must be noted that the more elaborate plants and programs we have described were found, as might be expected, in institutions for youthful offenders. Resources available in adult institutions were much more primitive—sometimes almost nonexistent. School programs for adults are not usually compulsory and sometimes are provided only during off-duty hours—often by teachers who are either volunteers or moonlighters. Correspondence programs are quite common in those correctional centers.

A new educational force is beginning to crack the walls of many adult institutions. It is the community college. Many of these have extended their instruction to inmates of correctional centers by providing regularly scheduled credit courses within the institutions, by offering special non-credit courses, by entering into the training of correctional staff, and by participating in education release programs for selected offenders. Because these community colleges are opening all over America, often on a county or regional basis, they frequently are even within commuting distance of remote correctional centers. Inmates can be transported to and from them without great inconvenience or cost.

Of course, not only the community colleges have entered into this partnership with corrections. Many four-year colleges and universities have also. We observed a most enterprising program of higher education where Pennsylvania State University and the Rockview Penitentiary have joined in a program called "Project Newview."

The educational program has two main components. First, there is a two-year curriculum. This is nondegree but results in the awarding of a certificate. It is designed to take six terms or two academic years for completion. Courses in three areas (landscape design, ornamental horticulture, and general educational electives) are taught both at the institution and at the university's main campus at State College. All participants in this program reside within the institution and are bused as a group to the campus for the classes given there. Each man takes courses in all three areas of study. Selection for the two-year program requires at least normal intelligence and interest in the subject areas which were selected to afford potential employment with governmental agencies, educational and state institutions, private agencies (nursery, landscape, building, etc.), and self-employed businesses.

Secondly, there is a four-year program. This is a full-time activity designed for the achievement of the bachelor's degree. To participate an inmate must meet the university's matriculation standards. Usually men are admitted to the program when they have about two years remaining prior to their minimum sentence parole date. There are four distinct phases in the program.

(1) In-institution. Initial general studies and remedial work is done by the men on the institution grounds. Classes are taught and work is supervised by Pennsylvania State faculty. Special carrels and study schedules are provided for participants.

(2) Halfway House. Within one term of parole date the men are transferred to a setting on Rockview grounds, but not behind the fence. These men live in a six-man farm house and are bused to and from the institution to the university campus. They are "free" all day on campus to go about their academic work and at night are unsupervised at the halfway house except for a daily count and occasional check.

(3) Community Residence. During the term in which they are paroled, the men are transferred to a group residence at State College. Except for one count each day, the routine and activities of these men are indistinguishable from other university students. During this term, they are usually paroled and then make plans for continuing their education. The "community" aspect of the program will be discussed in greater detail.

(4) After-care. This office, located on campus, provides coordination of all university student services, personal counseling, and fiscal management for all students in the program beyond the in-institutional phase.

We were impressed by these and other educational programs which we observed. However, probably because of my fairly long experience of working within a correctional institution, I find myself with a gnawing feeling about them. All these programs, even the best, are grafted upon confinement. Confinement, I believe, is an enormously counterproductive experience—so counterproductive that it neutralizes, even vitiates, the combined effectiveness of the good people and sometimes excellent facilities.

There are
many attempts
to undo the
counter-productiveness
of confinement.

Treatment Approach   Many correctional administrators have chosen or have taken on by default a clinical or psychotherapeutic model as a basic method of treatment. It seems to be based upon a premise that the offender has psychological problems and that those problems contribute to his/her antisocial behavior. This method may involve the individual in a one-to-one relationship with a treatment person or it may be a group endeavor. In either case, the responsible staff person is usually professionally trained—most frequently in social work, the ministry, psychology, or psychiatry. Variations of the clinical model have evolved which utilize paraprofessionals. These include college-educated counselors who carry case loads and who "treat" the more circumstantial manifestations of an inmate's behavior. The inmate, for example, is expected to relate to the counselor regarding institutional problems, program choices, and parole planning. Specially chosen guards have also been assigned to this role as well as to the task of leading group counseling sessions. Recently, inmates and former inmates have been engaged as counselors and group leaders.

The girls' institutions at Macon, Georgia, and Waynesburg, Pennsylvania, are examples of programming which is clinically oriented. In both of these institutions, the principal employees—superintendent, supervisors, and counselors—are predominantly professionally trained social workers. Both, of course, have other rehabilitation methods such as academic and vocational education, but the core of their program is clinical with individual and group social work as its principal treatment skills. Waynesburg was designed so that the case workers are removed from the mainstream of institutional activity. Their offices are located in the administration building several hundred yards away from the cottages, school, and recreation space. The model was one that was popular in social work a few years ago with its workers ensconced in a professional-looking office to which the client came for help an hour or so each week. As I point out later this is an archaic approach to treatment—particularly if treatment is viewed as a dynamic, fluid process.

We saw similar examples all over the country. At Bordentown and Yardville, in New Jersey, separate "treatment" buildings provide space for psychologists, psychiatrists, case workers, and counselors. At Marion, Illinois, the counselors' offices were originally located, we were told, outside the prison's perimeter. Security made it impossible for most inmates to get to the offices. At Hagerstown and Ionia, the counseling staffs were originally in school buildings that were open during the school day. Even at brand new Leesburg, the "treatment" and counseling offices are removed from where the people are. There has been a noticeable shift that now requires the clinician or counselor to be where the inmates are—to be available. As a result, space in housing units designed for other purposes is being altered to serve the treatment purpose. The small libraries in each cottage at Waynesburg, for example, are now used for counseling and group interaction. In other institutions we saw closets, dayrooms, bedrooms, and guards' stations that have been converted for group or individual counseling.

This newer model results in an increased involvement on the part of the clinical professional who becomes part of a treatment team in which he is a co-member with the guard, the cottage parent, and the teacher. All are intimately involved together in the offender's total institutional experience. The design implication for this shift was at first quite insignificant. It was merely to provide space in the housing unit for the counselor's individual and group therapy. But out of the immediacy of the constant interaction among professional staff, custodial personnel, and inmates evolved new forms of treatment which revolutionized the role of the therapist and made dramatic new architectural demands. One of these new treatment techniques is "reality" therapy.

Reality therapy demands a continuous accounting by each inmate to his peers and to his counselors for his behavior. It is premised on a belief that an inmate must learn to accept responsibility for his words and actions. Standards of behavior are defined by the group. Anyone whose behavior does not measure up to those standards has to come before members of the group to explain his conduct.

This kind of treatment also makes demands on institutional design. For example, it is quite difficult to be irresponsible in the cagelike prisons which dot our land. Moreover, it is almost impossible for groups to confront irresponsibility when there is no natural place for groups to come together.

Behavior Modification   Behavior modification as a treatment approach is an application of principles derived from psychological learning theory. In simplest terms, it holds that behavior — good or bad — is learned. The treatment itself is directed toward unlearning old or learning new behavior. Its unique importance, so far as its application in correctional institutions is concerned, is its emphasis on positive rather than negative reinforcement. Prisons have always operated on a belief that behavior depends upon its consequences, but historically the traditional application of that principle has been negative. Behave or suffer the lash. Conform or go to the Hole. Adjust or lose parole. Punishment has always taken precedence over reward. Behavior modification programs, as we saw them in several new institutions throughout the country, provide a clearly defined system of rewards as well as punishments with the emphasis, it seemed to us, on the positive (reward) consequences of acceptable behavior rather than the punishment of unacceptable conduct.

At the Karl Holton School for Boys, which is part of a large complex for youth near Stockton, California, behavior modification is the principal program emphasis. The authorities there have designed what they hope to be a total experience for the residents which will bring about a cessation or significant reduction of antisocial behavior, while helping to develop nondelinquent behavior and skills. There appear to be two principal elements in this total program.

The first is the assignment of specific measurable goals for each lad. Among them are management tasks such as mealtime behavior, group movements, and classroom conduct. But, in time, achievement goals are also set for each boy. These may include the overcoming of educational deficiencies, development of vocational skills, and changing of specific behavior manifestations — for example, assaultiveness. In short, a treatment plan is developed for each inmate.

The second program element is the reward system by which desired behavior is reinforced. At Holton a token economy system has been developed. Each youth is issued a bank book and is paid, in scrip, for his performance. He earns a minimum daily wage plus additional "Behavior Change Units" for accomplishing goals included in his treatment plan. With these token payments he may purchase amenities such as increased recreation, a copy of *Playboy*, or a great number of other privileges. He can even use them to reduce his length of stay. The tokens which he receives for desired behavior and achievement thus become his specific positive reinforcers. On the other hand, they also become negative reinforcers because the lad can be fined. For example, a fight may cost him $50.

There are design implications that grow out of behavior modification theory. The Kennedy Youth Center in West Virginia is a case in point because there a resident may use his accumulated scrip to purchase, among other things, improved accommodations. He has a choice of three—a cubicle in an open ward, a Spartan room, or more comfortable and better located quarters to which he will hold the key. For behavior modification to have optimal benefits, the facilities must be flexible. They must be able to accommodate the changing activities that become available to inmates as their "income" increases. Moreover, the living units should be small and intimate enough to facilitate interaction between inmates and staff.

Most programs which we saw were developed after the building was constructed so the program had to be adapted to the facility—many times with difficulty. This may be forever necessary, however, because many treatment programs come and go in fadlike fashion. The behavior modification programs which we saw are only in an experimental stage though some of the practitioners don't talk as if they are.

The North Carolina Youth Center at Morganton (not to be confused with the Kennedy Center at Morgantown discussed above) is an example of a building designed for one purpose and altered, without major structural changes, for a behavior modification program. We have already described it as a 16-story high-rise located at the foothills of the Smoky Mountains. The several floors devoted to housing are, with the exception of the segregation unit, essentially similar in layout. The 14th floor, for example, is used for reception. It contains a large but sparsely furnished dayroom and individual outside cells with prison-type doors. Each cell contains a built-in cabinet, desk, chair, and bed, but no toilet. This modest room is the irreducible minimum that is every inmate's basic right at Morganton.

The resident can progress from the frugal existence of the 14th floor, with its sterile physical and social environment, to a more enriched living experience on the 5th floor. On the 13th floor the prison doors have been replaced by wooden ones. A television set and a ping-pong table are added to the dayroom on the 12th floor (and dessert to the menu). The 10th floor has curtains, tape recorders, and increased privileges; the 9th allows personal radios and longer evening recreation; the 8th introduces more personal equipment such as reading lamps and a telephone booth. By the time a youth has progressed to the 5th floor, he has more comfortable furniture, keys to his room, attractive china and cutlery, and a wide series of options related to recreation, visiting, eating, canteen usage, and dress.

We have already remarked more than once that corrections has been facile in incorporating into its modus operandi the latest in theories, techniques, and even fads from the behavioral sciences. Often corrections' commitment to them has been superficial, and there has been little or no evaluation of the results. It appears that behavior modification is currently the "in" treatment method among corrections' avant-garde. In the past, Goddard, then Freud, and others were the high priests of correctional psychology. Today it is Skinner, and the federal government is currently constructing a monument to him and his theories at Butner, North Carolina. It should be completed by the fall of 1973 and will be called the Behavioral Research Center of the Federal Bureau of Prisons. At Butner, the buildings in which the residents will live will not be called cellblocks, housing units, residences, cottages, or any of the other appellations familiar to corrections. They will be called "Behavior Modification Program Units." Voila!

There will be four different designs for the behavior modification units, so that different programs can be developed for distinct subgroups of offenders. Corrections has always given lip service to differential treatment, but often the approach has not been very sophisticated. In recent years, behavior scientists, especially Marguerite Warren of California and Herbert Quay of Philadelphia, have developed new methods of classifying offenders and new treatment strategies based upon them. Basic to their work is the very obvious, but often ignored, fact that any specific treatment program may be beneficial to one offender but detrimental to another.

The application of a sophisticated program of differential treatment makes demands upon building design. We saw at the Kennedy Center a beginning attempt to provide housing units that will respond to the specific needs of the different types of offenders. The federal people who run Morgantown chose Dr. Quay's approach to differential treatment as their model, and they have identified five behavior categories (BC): inadequate-immature (BC1), neurotic-conflicted (BC2), unsocialized-aggressive or psychopathic (BC3), subcultural (BC4), and a hybrid called (BC5). A methodology has been developed for classifying the youth into one of these categories.

Just as each behavior category defines the characteristics of the offender, it also spells out the desired characteristics of the staff persons who will be assigned to work with the individuals in each category, the objectives in each person's treatment program, and the requirements of his physical environment. Some living units, for example, should provide for the physical demands of a BC3 (aggressive) while other units respond to the less vigorous requirements of a BC2 (neurotic). At Morgantown, we found that the housing units did not particularly fit the always changing population. Each unit serves 52 youths, but BC1's, BC2's, BC3's, and BC4's don't come in groups of 52. There might, for example, be 97 BC1's and only 27 BC2's. Thus the carefully devised differential treatment program was being eroded by the physical realities of the place.

We found some inmate talk to be laughable, except that it was not funny. I refer to the kind of bragging that went on about some behavior categories. Apparently one bragged about his manliness if he was, say, a BC3 or BC4. The BC1's tried to hide their identity, at least to us. Some even took up fighting, we were told, just to prove that they were not passive or inadequate. One fellow told us that he was originally classified as a BC1 (inadequate-immature) and ended up as a BC3, the aggressive type. Another lad, almost in anguish, put it this way, "Mr. Nagel, I don't want to be a BC1. I don't want to be a BC5. I don't want to be a BC3. I just want to be me." Recently the Kennedy Center has become coeducational. This might have unimagined effect on the classification system.

Without attempting to critically evaluate the behavior modification approach, we must question any method which is accepted religiously as the answer to all our problems. This causes people to address themselves rigidly to the approach with little concern for its applicability to the specific population. I have seen too many dyed-in-the-wool Freudians who today are behavior modifiers. The question is, what will they be tomorrow?

Transactional Analysis

Another of the newer psychological techniques that we observed during our travels is called "transactional analysis" which is based upon a process developed by Eric Berne. Basic to the theory is the assumption that each individual is, within himself, three persons: a parent, an adult, and a child. The technique utilizes "games," "psychodrama," and "script analysis" to reveal one's hidden thoughts and motives and to help him to understand which of his three persons controls his behavior and life style. The goal, then, is for the resident to get a clearer understanding of his three ego states (persons) and hopefully develop spontaneity and a capacity for intimacy. Having achieved these things, it is said, he is less likely to be delinquent.

This kind of treatment makes enormous demands on the environment. The correctional center must provide space for small group sessions for that is the primary therapeutic tool. It must also provide ample offices for individual counseling because that is an essential backup tool. There must be easy movement between the small community of the therapy group and the larger community of the whole institution for the inmate to test himself outside the intimacy of his primary associates. Optimally, it will also provide links to the still greater community outside the institution.

We saw forms of transactional analysis at the federal penitentiary at Marion, Illinois, where a psychiatrist has established a small therapeutic community within that maximum security prison. The community is called Asklepicion, and it is an exceedingly evangelical cluster of people who appear to be involved in what, for them, is an important, even messianic, experience. The O. H. Close School which is part of a larger youth complex near Stockton, California, is utilizing transactional analysis as its basic treatment method.

We should point out that our task was to look at new correctional institutions and to describe the state of correctional architecture. Needless to say, we had to examine the various programs for which buildings are merely settings. However, we had neither the inclination nor the time to critically evaluate the kind of complex, even mysterious, programs which we observed. Fortunately some programs are being carefully scrutinized, and in time we will know more about their effectiveness. At Stockton the success of transactional analysis at O. H. Close is being carefully compared to that of behavior modification at the sister institution, Karl Holton. Both are being compared to traditional programs in other California institutions. Evaluative research has been built into the two federal experimental programs at Marion and Morgantown, and the new Butner institution has research as its middle name. Hopefully, we may soon know whether corrections has, at long last, found some solutions to its perplexing tasks. We recognize, however, that behavioral scientists and psychologists have been trying to evaluate the effectiveness of treatment approaches for three decades now with questionable results.

Medical Services

It is difficult to generalize about the facilities and services for medical and dental care that we observed, other than to say that to us laymen the quality of the facilities seemed to exceed that of the services. In the larger institutions we saw expensive hospitals complete with outpatient departments, offices, dental suites, laboratories, diet kitchens, pharmacies, nurses' stations, and also examining, x-ray, hydrotherapy, operating and sterilizer rooms. They seemed very complete, professional, and sanitary. But in general they were very underused. There appear to be at least two major explanations for the underuse. Most institutions that we visited were located at very isolated sites. The surrounding towns, usually small, had trouble enough finding doctors and other medical service personnel without sharing

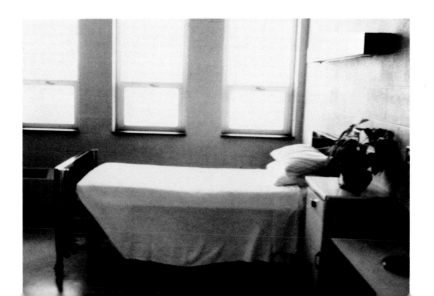

them with the big state prison located nearby. Also doctors are very expensive, and correctional budgets are not competitive. Therefore, many institutions provide little more than routine medical services. More complicated medical procedures, especially surgery, cannot be offered in spite of the availability of quite adequate physical resources. The staff for postoperative care, for example, is usually not available even when the surgeon can be scheduled. As a result we saw operating rooms in which no operation had ever been performed, laboratories where no test had been made, and sterilizing rooms in which the equipment was still in boxes. But even more sad to say, we saw places where medical services were provided by inmate "medics." We were especially appalled by our observations of medical services in the prison system of Alabama. In that state, they have concentrated their medical services, such as they are, in one institution. Inasmuch as the state's other prisons are located vast distances away, it is difficult, if not impossible, to provide for more than the most routine medical services. One prison doctor with whom we talked bewailed the problems he faces in getting medical services from a prison medical center over 200 miles away. He vividly described his anguish as he drove that long distance with a sitting patient critically in need of surgery. Other employees of that institution told us that inmates quite frequently slice their Achilles tendon, and that repair is frequently done without anesthesia. We were unable, due to the limitations of our mission and our time, to ascertain the veracity of the horror stories we heard at this and other prisons. However, as I write this (October 5, 1972), an Associated Press dispatch from Alabama seems to confirm our most unhappy findings. It says:

U. S. District Judge Frank M. Johnson, Jr. ordered prison authorities in Alabama to take immediate steps to provide adequate medical care for all inmates. . . .

"Unsupervised prisoners, without formal training, regularly pull teeth, screen sick-call patients, dispense as well as administer medication, including dangerous drugs, take X-rays, suture, and perform minor surgery," Judge Johnson said.

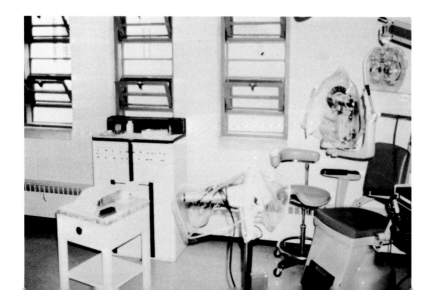

Evidence showed a "chronic shortage of medical supplies throughout" the prison system. "Rags have been used as a substitute" for bandages and for gauze sponges during surgery.

"Not only are prescription drugs frequently unavailable, especially those for relieving pain," Johnson said, "but simple items such as aspirin and antacids have been lacking in some prisons for weeks at a time."

Johnson, in a 12-page decision and an accompanying four-page order spelling out what prison officials must do, said penal authorities "have clearly abused their discretion" in denying proper medical treatment to the almost 4,000 inmates.

We note that other state and federal courts have recently abandoned their traditional "hands off" role in regard to medical services and have brought in findings against states which are tantamount to neglect.

In our travels we noted a movement to concentrate the major medical services of a prison system in one institution. While we were in Florida, we observed the construction of a new central medical facility at Lake Butler. It will serve the entire Florida system in spite of the fact that Lake Butler is a tiny hamlet located great distances from the major centers of medicine—Miami, Tampa, Jacksonville, and Tallahassee. We were told that Georgia plans a similar central medical facility at its Reception and Diagnostic Center at Jackson, another very small town. Fortunately, that location is only 60 or so miles from the great medical complexes in Atlanta.

Many of the prison doctors with whom we talked advised against building prison hospitals at all. They, and increasing numbers of administrators, are depending upon the medical resources of the nearest city or medical center. They recommend that correctional institutions be equipped and staffed to offer only routine health care while more intensive treatment should be provided by state-funded security wards at nearby community hospitals. Many jurisdictions now are taking that route toward more adequate medical services. The chief physician at Marion told us that the federal system is increasingly using the community. At almost all institutions for women and juvenile offenders that we visited, major medical services were being provided in the community hospitals.

Summation   In the very beginning of this section on correctional programs, we observed that, in the two centuries of the history of corrections, one treatment concept after another has evolved and been absorbed into the system in continuous efforts to overcome the inherent weaknesses of confinement.

There are still numerous institutions and systems that have not passed beyond the very primitive. In fact we saw many such examples of benighted penology, even though our itinerary was designed so that we would observe only the most modern of our correctional facilities.

I worked for many years in what was regarded as one of the most progressive correctional institutions in the country. We were pioneers in the development of several treatment techniques which were, at the time of my employment there, considered very advanced. They included group therapy, social casework, group counseling, education for life, hypnotherapy, and others.

We went far and wide to recruit eager and competent psychiatrists, psychologists, social caseworkers, teachers, and other skilled people; and they worked with imagination and devotion. We developed an institution with a high morale, a great sense of purpose, and a flexible approach to the treatment of crime and delinquency. Many inmates, over the years, attested to me that imprisonment at Bordentown had been meaningful. Just recently I spent a day discussing corrections with a group of professionals at one of our great universities. One of these professionals looked familiar to me, and I asked him where I had known him before. He said, "Bordentown. I was there in 1949 and '50." I felt some element of pride that this intelligent man had found success, but I had no right to that pride because he told me that since Bordentown he had been in a half dozen other prisons. In fact, he had spent most of those 22 years in somebody's jail.

In spite of all our efforts during those exciting years, we did not appreciably change the recidivist rate. During the years that I was there (1949-60) we made one careful comparison of recidivism over two five-year periods to determine postinstitutional success and failure. Though staff efforts and programs multiplied during the period, our success rate did not change appreciably. We had a more humane institution, a more responsive one, a more caring one – and all that made it worthwhile – but we did not have a more successful one in terms of reduced recidivism.

Our experience was not unique. Careful researchers, such as Wolfgang, Conrad, Wilkins, and, most recently, Martinson, have reported that few, if any, correctional programs have noticeably affected the recidivist rate. Martinson, in fact, reviewed 231 accepted studies of correctional treatment published since 1945. The results are available in an 800-page volume entitled *The Treatment Evaluation Survey*. The evidence from that survey indicates that the present array of correctional treatments has no appreciable effect – positive or negative – on the rates of recidivism.

Martinson echoes the conclusion articulated two decades ago by a gifted reporter and observer of American prisons,

John Bartlow Martin. In his book, *Break Down the Walls,* written after the prison riots of 1952 and '53, he wrote that professional people in corrections had devised a dangerous myth — that of institutional treatment. He said that it is a myth because it is not true that prison can rehabilitate. He said that rehabilitation is a pie-in-the-sky idea. "We appear to believe," he said, "that if we provide the stainless steel kitchen, the schools and shops and toilets, one day rehabilitation will descend upon the inmate, like manna." Another gifted reporter, Ben Bagdikian, wrote practically the same thing 20 years later in his noteworthy book, *Shame of the Prisons* (1972). This was written after another series of deadly riots — Attica, Holmesburg, and Rahway.

Many scholars have tried to understand why institutionalization seems not to work. Haynes, in 1948, found the inmate community to be distinctly antisocial and that it worked against the goals of the larger society and thereby against rehabilitation efforts. Reimer, even earlier, noted that inmates acquire status in terms of their antiauthority reactions to the prison situation and that therefore the behavior of convicts is determined by convicts themselves. Clemmer observed that the prisoner, through assimilation or acculturation, takes on the delinquent folkways, mores, customs, and general culture of the penitentiary. McCorkle and Korn conclude that the prison represents, in fact is, the ultimate in social rejection and that its inmates develop increased antisocial values in order to "reject the rejectors." Other serious investigators — Sykes, Goffman, Cloward, Schrag — have noted that prison subcultures work powerfully to subvert even the most conscientious of treatment efforts.

Gaylin, Weber, and others have noted another phenomenon that contributes to the failure of the prison and to many institutions for youth. When in these places, large numbers of human beings are placed in a closed society in which the many have to be controlled by a few officials. This creates special counterproductive pressures.

In the outside society, unity and a sense of community contribute to personal growth. In the society of prisoners, unity and community must be discouraged lest the many overwhelm the few. In the world outside, leadership is an ultimate virtue. In the world inside, leadership must be identified, isolated, and blunted. In the competitiveness of everyday living, assertiveness is a characteristic to be encouraged. In the reality of the prison, assertiveness is equated with aggression, and repressed. Other qualities considered good on the outside — self-confidence, pride, individuality — are eroded by the prison experience into self-doubts, obsequiousness, and lethargy. In short, individuality is obliterated and the spirit of man is broken in the spiritlessness of obedience.

AN
ENQUIRY

INTO THE EFFECTS OF

PUBLIC PUNISHMENTS

A Bad Night

U P O N

C R I M I N A L S

A N D U P O N

S O C I E T Y.

at the

READ IN THE SOCIETY FOR PROMOTING POLITICAL
ENQUIRIES, CONVENED AT THE HOUSE OF
HIS EXCELLENCY

Holiday Inn

BENJAMIN FRANKLIN, Esq.

IN PHILADELPHIA, MARCH 9th, 1787.

By BENJAMIN RUSH, M.D.

PROFESSOR OF CHEMISTRY IN THE UNIVERSITY OF
PENNSYLVANIA.

" Accuftomed to look up to thofe Nations from whom we have
" derived our Origin, for our Laws, our Opinions, and our Man-
" ners; we have retained, with undiftinguifhing Reverence, their
" Errors, with their Improvements; have blended, with our Public
" Inftitutions, the Policy of diffimilar Countries; and have grafted,
" on an Infant Commonwealth, the Manners of ancient and cor-
" rupted Monarchies." *Preface to the Laws of the Society for Political Enquiries.*

PHILADELPHIA, PRINTED:

LONDON, REPRINTED FOR C. DILLY, IN THE
POULTRY.

M,DCC,LXXXVII.

A Bad Night at the Holiday Inn

During 1972 I had the privilege of serving on the Corrections Task Force of the National Commission on Criminal Justice Standards and Goals. Its report is scheduled for release almost simultaneously with the publication of this book. The task force was chaired by Judge Joe Frasier Brown of Texas and included some of the most distinguished correctional officials and scholars in the country. At a meeting in Atlanta we became involved in a most spirited debate about the future of the correctional institution. Most of the members argued for additional alternatives, more humane surroundings, better staffing, increased treatment, specific prisoner's rights, and larger appropriations. I pleaded for the abandonment of the prison. I lost, and that night in a motel room I wrote the following letter to many of my fellow task force members:

Dear Friends:

After the Task Force meeting today, I flew to the far western part of North Carolina to visit the brand new 16 story high-rise prison which opens tomorrow. Built miles from anywhere on literally thousands of acres of largely unoccupied state land, it rises majestically, challenging the Smoky Mountains which surround it.

There I saw the newest in American penology and heard the most modern of Skinnerian logic. Then I went to my Holiday Inn and tried to escape from it all in slumber. But I couldn't sleep. I kept thinking about our meeting in Atlanta and a historical fantasy commenced to consume me. The hollow table around which we sat at Atlanta became round. Judge Brown began to look like an Anglican Bishop. Bob's short hair took the form of a powdered wig. Edith's yellow suit turned to the plain brown of an 18th century Quaker, and there we were in the Black Horse Tavern just across the square from Independence Hall in Philadelphia. It was 1790. Here is my fantasy, dictated as I dreamt it that night in my Holiday Inn bed.

. . . . .

Ebenezer Vail felt honored to be one of the group who had been invited to the Black Horse Tavern for this important meeting.

Bishop White was presiding. The Revolution had brought all kinds of changes and he was still trying to get used to being called an Episcopalian instead of an Anglican. Everybody respected the Bishop. He was truly a good man and thought people were made in the image of God and should not, therefore, have their hands cut off, or their eyes burned out for stealing a pig or peeking at Widow Jones getting undressed. Not that he approved peeking.

Caleb Satherwaithe was there too. He was what some people called a powerful political figure. He had lots of contacts in the General Assembly. He knew how to use them too. Somewhere along the road he had become dedicated to the work of penal reform.

Professor Strawbridge was a very important force in the movement. No one knew just why he was so interested in the penal law, but inasmuch as he had but recently migrated to Pennsylvania from Georgia, some people whispered that he was the son of a transported convict, and that was his motivation.

Peggy Shipp was also present. This would have been unthinkable under ordinary circumstances, but the new republic was trying all sorts of unusual things, even including involving women in public matters. And Peggy Shipp was no usual woman. She had brains. After dinner when the men were sipping their brandy they would even admit that it was pleasant to look at her.

Jonathan Thomas was a strange one. He had a first class mind and was a stickler for things like definitions, and clarity, and proof. He was one of the new breed of public servants that the infant commonwealth had employed, and he was a capable one.

Other good and thoughtful people squeezed around the green-covered table. John Barlow, Prudence Jones, Jeremy Toothill, Dr. Benjamin Bush, and others. They all had one thing in common with Ebenezer Vail. They were bothered by the brutality of the punishments meted out by the law and wanted to present a series of recommendations for change to the General Assembly.

Ebenezer was not really as distinguished as the others, but he was often invited to meetings like this because he had such strong feelings on the subject. He had been an assistant public executioner, but not a very well-known one. Not being the intellectual type he found it hard to follow the detailed intricacies of Jonathan Thomas' complicated logic. Peggy Shipp's brilliant and disciplined mind overwhelmed him. Unlike the others he wasn't very proficient at writing and his infrequent efforts were usually simplistic and very poorly spelled. But like a few other former public executioners he retched at the sight of men getting their necks snapped or their hands chopped off. He fervently prayed that the new republic would find some substitute, and he came to this meeting with hope in his heart. It was 1790 and just possibly this would be the year that his fellow Americans might try to outlaw publicly sanctioned inhumanity.

What a meeting it was. Everyone wanted to do something but none seemed to agree on just what. Caleb thought that maybe you could retain capital and corporal punishment just for the dangerous offenders. This incensed Thomas who demanded that somebody tell him precisely what a dangerous offender is. This no one was able to do, to everybody's satisfaction, so the matter was dropped. Professor Strawbridge, who had great skill at formulating middle positions, suggested that we forget the dangerous offenders for a while and try to agree on what we should do with the lesser felons—those that stole pigs and watched

Widow Jones undress. Surely they didn't need to have their hands cut off and their eyes burned out. Toothill was worried by this. He wanted to know how public values would be affirmed.

Prudence thought that maybe we could just cut the fingers off instead of the whole hand. Cartwright, a progressive public executioner, thought Prudence's idea a good one. He even went further and suggested that the amputation be done on a clean white table instead of the dirty cutting block. Dr. Bush got really excited about the idea of sanitary amputations and went even further suggesting that a scalpel instead of a meat cleaver be used. For a moment it looked as if real progress was in the wind.

Ebenezer Vail couldn't take it any more. With more feeling than eloquence, more passion than reason he pleaded, "Cutting hands off is evil even if done with a scalpel. For God's sake, let's recommend that it be stopped."

Thomas was on his feet. "I reject words like 'evil.' Who says it's evil? The criminal code has authorized it since the dawn of civilization."

Peggy joined in. "It doesn't have to be evil. I know I could amputate a hand without any hurt to the offender." Ebenezer almost believed Peggy could, but he feebly added he felt it was still evil. He knew he couldn't cut his own sons' hands off and he didn't think the state should either.

Public Executioner Cartwright reminded Vail that times had changed since he (Vail) had been an assistant public executioner, and corporal and capital punishment should not, therefore, be condemned out of hand because of the methods of yesteryear. He added that better methods were on the horizon.

Poor Ebenezer was beaten, but he tried one last tack. He blurted out, "Cutting off hands, however you do it, is handicapping and, therefore, self-defeating." Barlow suggested that perhaps the handicapping aspects could be corrected by physical therapy which the new hospital on Spruce Street, America's first, was experimenting with.

Strawbridge, feeling Vail's despair, suggested that a phrase like "some good people question the efficacy of capital and corporal punishment" could be incorporated into the report. Caleb, with very great political acumen agreed, adding that to go any further would kill any chance of action from the legislature. "This is an election year, you know!"

Just then the door opened and in strode Ben Franklin. He apologized for being late explaining that as Postmaster General he had just resolved a problem concerning the Pony Express.

Bishop White quickly brought him up to date on all the discussion, to which Ben, considered a statesman by all, said, "You don't go far enough. I think we ought to go for broke." He added, "These are great and challenging times and Americans ought to set new heights for civilization everywhere." Doubting Thomas asked what the alternatives might be. Ben said that he didn't really know, but when he had been in Europe he had seen errant churchmen doing penance in cells at the monastery at Stuttgart. He added that an Englishman named Bentham proposed something similar for public offenders. To Thomas' further question Franklin answered that he just didn't know whether it would work, but what we are doing doesn't work either and moreover it is wicked.

Caleb Satherwaithe, sensitive to Franklin's stature and influence, reasoned that it was time to resolve the issue and he moved that the Pennsylvania Society memorialize the General Assembly to substitute imprisonment for capital and corporal punishment. Professor Strawbridge seconded and, with only Jonathan Thomas abstaining, the question was passed.

. . . . .

Just then the fantasy began to fade. The table became a hollow square again. Judge Brown had lost his ecclesiastical collar and Bob his powdered wig. Edith's dress again was bright yellow. And I looked and looked for the Ben Franklin among us, but he wasn't there.

Your sincere friend and well-wisher,

Bill

. . . . .

Of course this allegory refers to the historic moments nearly two centuries ago when the Quakers and their associates in Pennsylvania invented the penitentiary as a substitute for the barbarism of the then existing penology.

The prison has become the barbarism of today. After our trip around the nation my colleagues and I conclude that America, as we approach our country's bicentennial, must replace a penal system which has proved not only inhumane, but nonproductive.

In his First Inaugural Address, Thomas Jefferson said it well:

"We might as well require a man to wear still the coat which fitted him as a boy, as civilized society to remain ever under the regimen of their barbarous ancestors."

Where Now?

147

Where Now? For more than a decade, The American Foundation has wanted to upgrade correctional institutions. In fact it hired me as its director largely because at the very core I am a prison man. We undertook the study which led to this book because the foundation sought to contribute to a process that will lead toward improved jails, prisons, and juvenile facilities. Our president, board, and staff are inspired by essentially the same motives which drove John Howard from jail to jail throughout 18th century Europe seeking more sanitary, humane, and secure prisons in which to reform criminals.

My own professional self is rooted in that historic old agency, the Pennsylvania Prison Society, which invented the penitentiary. When I came out of the army after World War II, I went to work there. My first assignment was to visit convicts twice each week in the famous prison that the Prison Society had built a century and a quarter earlier. That Eastern State Penitentiary, as we have already remarked, was conceived by one of the great architects of the time, John Haviland. The very design of the prison he built was to be its principal agent of reform. The thick walls of its solitary cells were to insure penitence. I have been, then, very much a part of that persistent belief that it is possible to design a prison secure enough to quarantine the offender and human enough to contribute to his reformation.

Our odyssey took us to many of the new correctional institutions in America, and it was our hope — even our expectation — that in one or several of them we would see the elements of a correctional facility that could "safely hold" and at the same time "correct." My friend and mentor, Austin MacCormick, from time to time reminded us that it was people, not bricks and mortar, that made the good prison. He used to say that if he was given quality staff he could run a good prison in an old red barn. We hoped to find a "new red barn" designed in such a manner that the physical plant aided both the correctional and the security tasks.

We did see some imaginative and innovative architecture which tried quite valiantly to make less obvious the fact of confinement. Ornamental grilles and hollow blocks sometimes are used instead of bars. Internal walls are well glazed. Winding paths replace the long bleak corridors. Landscaped lawns and gardens cause some of the uninitiated to complain about "those country clubs for convicts." The grim stone wall is no longer built. The staff of these new facilities, many college trained, hustle at their innumerable, important tasks — supervising, teaching, counseling, training, treating, disciplining.

These are all enlightened changes. Yet in our conversations with inmates and staff alike and in our observations, we heard and saw the old preoccupation — control. We also observed deep mutual suspicion, great cynicism, and pervasive hypocrisy as the kept and the keepers played old games with each other while using the new sophisticated language of today's behavioral sciences. I have not worked in a prison since 1960, but it was as if everything had changed, yet nothing had changed. The institutions were new and shiny, yet in all their new finery they still seemed to harden everyone in them. Warm people enter the system wanting desperately to change it, but the problems they find are so enormous and the tasks so insurmountable that these warm people turn cold. In time they can no longer allow themselves to feel, to love, to care. To survive, they must become callous. The prison experience is corrosive for those who guard and those who are guarded. This reality is not essentially the product of good or bad architecture. It is the inevitable product of a process that holds troubled people together in a closed and limited space, depriving them of their freedom, their families, and their humanity while expecting a relatively few employees to guard, control, punish, and redeem them.

A half century ago a distinguished scholar and penologist, Frank Tannenbaum, undertook a task quite similar to ours. He examined many American prisons. Perhaps we traced his footsteps, for we ended precisely where he ended. His conclusion, written in 1922, could serve as ours:

We must destroy the prison, root and branch. That will not solve our problem, but it will be a good beginning. . . . Let us substitute something. Almost anything will be an improvement. It cannot be worse. It cannot be more brutal and more useless.

This should be the place to end this book. Having quoted Tannenbaum that we must destroy the prison, tear down the walls, the easy thing would be merely to add, "Amen." But there is the unanswered question, "What is that 'something' that we should substitute?" The prison, after all, is a substitute for capital and corporal punishment. Should we go back to them? Or is there a substitute for the substitute? Frankly, I don't know the full answer, but it seems to me there are some fairly obvious things that a rational society can do which would go far toward a solution. I shall discuss some of those which have occurred to me.

Moratorium on Construction

If this country is resolved to do something constructive about the crime problem, the immediate thing it must do is call a halt to the building of new prisons, jails, and training schools, at least for a time, while we plan and develop alternatives. We say this for two principal reasons. First, so long as we build, we will have neither the pressures nor the will to develop more productive answers. The correctional institution is the "out of sight, out of mind" response to the problem of crime. It gives us the impression that we have been strong and forceful in dealing with the criminal and thus with crime, while the fact is that we have merely swept the criminal and the problem under the rug. No study that I have ever seen, and there are many, provides any assurance that the prison reduces crime, while there is ample evidence that the fact of imprisonment is a heavy contributor to postrelease criminal activity. The prison provides only the illusion, not the reality, of protection against the criminal.

And secondly, jails and prisons are so very permanent. State prisons built over a century and a half ago are still in use in several states. Of the maximum security prisons currently operating, 56 were built in the 19th century. The famous Eastern State Penitentiary which we have referred to so often finally emptied its cells only last year. And still it sits there, indestructible, the cost of its razing prohibitive. Of the 69 county prisons and jails in my state of Pennsylvania, 20 (30%) are from 100 to 157 years old. An additional 35 were built prior to 1900 making a total of 55 (80%) constructed during the 19th century. In the United States as a whole, there are 25,000 jail cells and about the same number of prison cells which were built over a half century ago. If we were to begin to replace only those cells in American jails and prisons that were built more than 50 years ago, the price tag would exceed one billion, five hundred million dollars. The result would be that two or three more generations of Americans would be saddled with an expensive and counterproductive method of controlling crime. Moreover, additional thousands of offenders would be subjected to new variations of what we euphemistically call correctional treatment, but which is more frequently abject vegetation and sometimes severe brutalization.

To insure that we don't saddle future generations of Americans with any more prisons and jails than the absolute minimum necessary to protect, we must, it seems to me, stop all correctional construction at least until we have had reasonable time to plan and implement more promising and civilized alternatives. Some alternatives are already emerging and will be discussed in the subsequent pages of this book.

The protests against a moratorium on prison construction will come from every quarter. The hard liners will demand more, not less, cell space. The wardens and sheriffs (and few people recall that the greatest prison reformer of all times, John Howard, was a sheriff) will insist that these prisons and jails are already inadequate and overcrowded and must be supplemented or replaced. The idealists, sickened by the inhuman conditions in so many of our jails and prisons, will lobby for bright new replacements for intolerable places. The civil libertarians will argue that since our jails do not provide the basic protections and rights guaranteed by the Constitution, they should be replaced by new jails which do. Architects and contractors, with their edifice complexes, will be quick to oblige.

But this country of pragmatists must resist the pressures to build, or America will have delayed, and at great cost, the more reasonable solutions which must inevitably be worked out. We must, in the meantime, keep the lid on our Pandora's box of supposed correctional construction requirements.

A Public Health Approach

Historically, civilizations have viewed crime as a sickness, the causes of which lay within the criminal. Views as to the nature of that sickness have constantly been revised. Criminals were possessed by devils. They were perverse. They had biological, psychological, chemical, educational, moral, or social deficiencies. But whatever the nature of the sickness, the solution centered in doing something to the criminal. In different eras, the solutions were different. Execution, exile, mutilation, imprisonment, education, vocational training, psychiatry, and a plethora of other techniques have all, at one time or another, been tried.

All of these approaches are focused on the individual. They are in a very real way similar to traditional medicine. The doctor treats the patient for smallpox, diphtheria, yellow fever, tuberculosis. I suppose we would all be dead by now if medicine had remained exclusively patient-oriented. There is only so much success doctors can have in treating, after the fact, the effects of a killer disease. Great physicians and their allied scientists therefore sought to identify and then eliminate the source. Their efforts were not always popular. Superstition, ignorance, prejudice, and self-interest were often bigger problems than even the difficulties inherent in the scientific search for answers. Perhaps nowhere in literature are these impediments more dramatically portrayed than in Ibsen's *The Enemy of the People*. It will be recalled that the doctor in that story traced the outbreak of disease to the water supply of the village. The citizens of that resort town, threatened economically, turned vehemently against the doctor rather than correct the problem. This is the way we treat crime in this country.

There is danger, I know, in drawing too much of a parallel between the public health approach to the control of smallpox, for example, and the prevention of crime. Smallpox is, after all, an identifiable virus, while crime is anything that a legislative body says it is. The General Assembly in my state, for example, recently decided in all its wisdom that a woman who has been raped is guilty of a crime if she takes steps in Pennsylvania to abort the birth of the child who was conceived as a result.* In most other states, the same act would not be viewed as criminal.

Even though it may be dangerous to draw too much of a parallel between the public health approach to illness and

*Governor Shapp vetoed this abortion bill.

the prevention of crime, it is quite myopic not to consider the possible implications of such an approach. For example, it was impossible to work for years as I did in an institution which received an inordinate proportion of its inmates from one ward—the old central ward of Newark, New Jersey—and not to wonder about the pathology of that central ward.

If New York has many, many times the armed robberies of London, if Philadelphia has twoscore the criminal homicides of Vienna, if Chicago has more burglaries than all of Japan, if Los Angeles has more drug addiction than Western Europe, then must we not concentrate on the social and economic ills of New York, Philadelphia, Chicago, Los Angeles, America? That has not been our approach. We concentrate on locking up the offender while we ignore the underlying causes.

I am not a social architect nor the person to propose just how we, as a nation, should proceed in the task of eliminating the social and economic problems which plague our nation and which contribute so greatly to crime in our streets. I would suggest two reports as good places at which to begin. They are the *President's Report on Civil Disobedience* and the *Eisenhower Report* of the National Commission on Causes and Prevention of Violence. Both suggest that we must reorder our national priorities away from such overconcentration on protecting ourselves from supposed enemies on the outside while we strive toward improving the quality of life here at home. As the Eisenhower Commission stated it, "The time is upon us for a reordering of our national priorities and for a greater investment of resources in fulfillment of the two basic purposes of our Constitution—to establish justice and to insure domestic tranquility."

To insure this "domestic tranquility," the report insists that we as a nation must meet the goal of a decent home for every American, provide useful jobs for all who are able to work, and insure a basic income to those American families who cannot care for themselves. Further, we must strive toward the objective of insuring the fiscal vitality of urban government and provide additional innovative programs of opportunity for inner city youth. Finally, as the Kerner Commission insists, we must adopt as a national policy the all-out effort to eradicate the vestiges of racism in our country.

These are not popular tasks for a political leader to pursue. From my own five years on a governor's staff, I know that the great majority of Americans resent being taxed to support any of the above-mentioned objectives. Some pundits have even attributed much of the success of one party in the last national election to its ability not to be identified with such problems, thus attracting the support of "middle Americans." But the wave of violent crime will not recede until this nation moves further toward the solution of its problems of social and economic injustice.

Pluralism is as American as apple pie. Its roots lie in two of this country's most worthy traditions. Our forefathers were fearful of strong centralized authority and therefore placed operational responsibility for a wide range of governmental activities at the local level. Secondly, wherever possible, they chose to attack social problems through private rather than public auspices. Alexis de Tocqueville made note of both of these. In his *Democracy in America,* he compared our approach to the solution of social problems with that of Europe. In Europe, he noted, people faced with a problem petitioned the crown. In America they formed a private society.

In early America these private societies, including religious organizations, actually operated many of the social services including those which would today be called correctional services. In my state, Pennsylvania, for example, all the correctional facilities for juveniles were originally privately operated, and even today there are more children committed by the juvenile courts to private institutions than to public ones.

As our social problems became too huge for private philanthropy, many agencies relinquished operational activities to the public sector and undertook advocacy roles. They pushed their state toward providing adequate services. Unfortunately their thrust was often toward the creation of state agencies which paralleled their own interests. As a result the public social services, including correctional ones, have evolved as a categorical hodgepodge. In my state, Pennsylvania, as one example, the correctional system became a maze of different people and different agencies at different levels of government, each (to use the vernacular) "doing his own thing."

It became nearly 100 probation departments in 67 counties—some big, some small, some juvenile, some adult. It became two state agencies attempting to establish and supervise probation standards, each without power of enforcement, but offering "carrots" to stimulate change. It became a Board of Probation and Parole providing services to both "state" and "county" offenders. It became a Board of Pardons that determines clemency.

It became 70 county jails and prisons ranging in size from an average daily population of 1 to an average daily population of 1300. It became a Bureau of Corrections operating many institutions, ranging from small halfway houses to large maximum security prisons and including a facility for juveniles. It became a network of 20 unrelated and unsupervised juvenile detention homes servicing parts of the state while leaving juveniles in other areas to the uncertain mercies of the county jails.

It became a Bureau in the Department of Public Welfare that operates many youth development centers for forestry camps. It became 12 or more private institutions which,

Organization

according to their own dictates, admit or refuse to admit youngsters who have problems that are expressed in delinquent ways. It became a Governor's Justice Commission attempting to use the power of the federal "Safe Streets" dollar to bring order and change.

In short, corrections in Pennsylvania became an incomprehensible, inefficient, unproductive, and multileveled administrative maze. Moreover, it has, over the years, been a potpourri of interpersonal conflicts, interagency jealousies, and duplicating activities. Most tragically, it is such a loose federation of services that it is impossible to place responsibility on any one person or any one agency for corrections' past failures or for its future planning and direction.

The result, it seems to me, is a hopelessly fragmented correctional system that spends most of its dollar and manpower resources in maintaining a prison system that neither corrects nor protects while starving or ignoring those alternatives that promise both correction of the offender and protection to the public. Corrections in Pennsylvania then, because of its priorities and heavy dependence on antiquated prisons and because of its fragmented organization, affords our citizens only the shadow of protection, not the substance.

I dwell on Pennsylvania only because I know it best. We found the same fragmentation in other states. We also note that the President's Commission on Law Enforcement and the Administration of Justice (1967), the Advisory Commission on Intergovernmental Relations (1971), and the report of the National Commission on Criminal Justice Standards and Goals (1973) have all very forcefully stated that this fragmentation has outlived any usefulness which it may, at one time, have had.

In my view two drastic but necessary changes must be made. First, the states must each have a department of "cabinet" rank charged with the exclusive responsibility of planning and operating programs to reduce crime. That department, at a minimum, must have complete jurisdiction over all state field services—probation, parole, and other alternatives to confinement—and over all state-owned facilities for offenders—juvenile, youth, and adult.

In my view the legislature, the county commissioners, and the judiciary should seek to combine the probation services now offered by the counties with the probation and parole services of the state. This would enable the state to develop field services and other alternatives to confinement on a systematic and universal basis. This does not suggest that present probation staff in the counties would be replaced. Rather they would be incorporated into a larger system in which career opportunities would be enhanced.

Jails, too, should become part of the unified system. With a few notable exceptions, jails are the most inadequate and poorly financed part of the entire spectrum of correctional services. In my opinion, the county's function in the confinement process would be, at the very most, limited to pretrial detention. All other institutionalized offenders should be the responsibility of the state.

This may sound as if I am proposing removing corrections from the community. Not so. I am convinced that corrections must be locally operated. I am also convinced, however, that it must be centrally administered and financed.

Perhaps this all sounds quite obtainable, and reasonable people working on three distinguished commissions to which I have already referred urged this kind of unification. The chief objections come from the bureaucracies where diverse leaders energetically fight most proposals to unify corrections. I hate to say it, but we seem to have precisely the fragmented system many of us in corrections want, because we prefer to remain big fish in our little stagnating ponds. We use our muscle to rally support for the perpetuation of an archaic and counterproductive status quo. Bureaucracies— federal, state, and local—all over this nation are fighting the same self-serving rearguard actions that perpetuate the very fragmentation which objective commissions decry.

The second necessary change is that the legislatures of the different states, in their directions to their correctional agencies, should mandate the phased early closing of all the megaprisons and replace them as far as public safety permits with alternatives to confinement such as we will discuss later on. I do not suggest this out of any inordinate sympathy for the offender, but out of a growing conviction that our present efforts are proving counterproductive. Rather than protecting society from the ravages of crime, our present penal system contributes to the increase of crime.

For these offenders who, for one reason or another, are too dangerous for community programs, we may have to— over the years—construct a network of small correctional facilities in the towns and cities from which the offender comes and to which he will return. No longer can we tolerate the Atticas—huge and remote—where rural white guards, with their "nigger sticks," lord over city blacks, totally incapable of comprehending the differences between their own life style and aspirations and those of their black, city-bred charges.

As the reader may already conclude from the foregoing, it is difficult to conceive of any social problem area more in need of coordinated and uniform planning than that of crime and delinquency. This country's juvenile and criminal justice system is so complex and the interrelationships among its components so varied that even loyal supporters

Planning for Criminal Justice

view the system as an incomprehensible administrative maze. As we have already noted, correctional services have developed more by default than by design. They may be centralized at the state level, decentralized in cities and counties, or shared by the federal, state, county, and city governments in an almost infinite number of permutations. On every level of service, the question of integrated planning arises. The need for full-scale coordination is acute.

To overcome the fragmentation of the correctional system and to avoid the dissipation of energies and meager resources, effective relationships must be established among the various components of the criminal justice system — a system which thus far continues to function in considerable social and political isolation. Beyond these essential requirements, however, lies the need for well-defined objectives, definitions and standards, appropriate techniques for crime prevention and correction, careful allocation of resources, and meticulous research and program designs. Such requirements perforce suggest that planning activities be coordinated to the highest possible degree. Uniform state planning is probably the *sine qua non* for optimal planning results.

Such planning, however, may remain a long-range goal for many of the states in view of the competing value orientations that characterize American society. On one hand, there is a preference for a rational approach to social problems which stresses the application of science and technology in an integrated and coordinated way. On the other hand, there is the desire to disperse centers of authority and to defer the decision-making to the level of the local community. Given the reality of this value conflict, social planning in criminal justice will either need to compromise and accommodate these concerns or require an impetus from a *vis major* to pursue the more rational state-planning approach.

My associates and I who traveled the United States to observe correctional institutions profess no great knowledge about the intricacies of criminal justice planning. We have, however, been working with the Law Enforcement Assistance Administration in its efforts to rationalize the correctional planning process, and I have also served on the Corrections Task Force of the National Commission on Criminal Justice Standards and Goals. In both of these activities, we have been brought into close relationship with a remarkable group of planners at the University of Illinois centered at the National Clearinghouse for Criminal Justice Planning and Architecture. They have developed a model for criminal justice planning which we applaud. Their model uses an open-end approach and unites in a common planning effort the law enforcement, judiciary, and corrections branches with community resources. In accordance with its conceptual scheme of socialization and reintegration, the methodology represents a comprehensive and systematic approach to the planning of state, regional, and community correctional systems in which institutionalization is seen as the *last*, not the first, dispositional alternative.

Although the model recognizes the continued need for the incarceration of the convicted, unusually refractory offender, nevertheless, because of the many inadequacies of our knowledge and our techniques in treatment, it recommends such drastic measures for only a few, and it uses greater selectivity and sophistication in the application of crime control and correctional methods. The same principles apply for the pretrial detainee. Sufficient evidence has now accumulated to show that the criminal justice system is overburdened with persons needlessly and inappropriately detained. Restraint practices are weighted disproportionately towards the detention of those members of society who are part of ethnic or minority groups and who are unemployed, undereducated, and disenfranchised. In addition, there is the dangerous and crime-producing mixture of persons who represent substantial threats to community safety with those who pose minimal risk or none at all. The result is the tense and damaging atmosphere peculiar to most jails today.

While it remains within the general boundaries of the legal framework and continues to protect the safety of the public, the model identifies, for any given target area, the probable minimum of offenders for whom detention must be provided. It further identifies the probable maximum of offenders for whom alternatives to incarceration must be utilized. A series of program linkages are then provided, stressing the divestment of social, medical, and moral problem cases from the criminal justice system and shifting the emphasis and resources from institutional to community corrections. If the current overloads of the system are to be overcome, social welfare cases and cases in need of medical and psychiatric assistance must be removed from it. Moreover, the criminal justice system is singularly ineffective in dealing with the mentally ill, the alcoholic, and the drug addict. We know today that applying criminal sanctions to such persons only exacerbates their problems and contributes heavily to the revolving door syndrome that characterizes our jails and penal institutions.

The planning model makes similar recommendations for the divestment of juveniles in need of care and supervision who have not committed criminal offenses. Their removal from the aegis of juvenile justice to more appropriate youth service agencies—family services or the newly emerging youth service bureaus—represents a much more realistic approach to the prevention of juvenile delinquency and avoids the criminalizing influence of stigmatization and isolation.

The model identifies a host of community-based correctional programs which relate to identified offender needs. It recognizes that the traditional institutional approach, with its coercive settings and inadequate programs, has failed to an impressive degree.

The banishment of offenders into isolated institutions, warehousing them in crippling idleness under conditions of stark deprivation and anonymous brutality, insure failure. Such practices are clearly self-defeating.

In summary, the model provides a validated approach to comprehensive planning in crime control by which current public and private agencies and institutions can be transformed into a more responsive criminal justice system.

Revising the Criminal Code

Earlier in this book it was noted that the Pennsylvania General Assembly had passed legislation this year which would have made it a crime for a woman to undergo an abortion following an act of rape or incest. It was vetoed by the governor after heated pressure from advocates pro and con. The author of that bill introduced in the same term a second piece of legislation. It would have made premarital or extramarital sex a criminal act. Another legislator in opposing this bill said, "He who is without guilt cast the first aye." The vote of "aye" by 72 legislators caused one newspaper to state editorially that it is comforting to know that our General Assembly is so pure.

We have an insufferable amount of criminal activities in this country which are indeed evil in themselves — murder, rape, assault, arson, robbery. They threaten our very society. Since the dawn of history there have been universal criminal sanctions against such acts. The protection of life, limb, and property requires that their perpetrators be not only condemned, but punished.

Since 1900 the great thrust of the changes to our criminal codes has not been to protect us against these crimes that are evil in themselves. Our legislatures have been working day and night to protect us against acts which are evil because legislators have decreed them to be evil. Legislating morality has become their special passion. As a result our criminal codes are clogged with laws which would, if they were fully enforced, make criminals out of most, if not all, of us. We have literally thousands of sanctions against drinking, pot smoking, gambling, vagrancy, disorderly conduct, abortion, and a wide variety of sexual activities between consenting adults including, in many cases, between husband and wife. These statutes are based not on harm done to others, but on legislatively declared moral standards that condemn behavior in which the only one hurt is the person so behaving, if indeed even he is hurt.

Many of the acts condemned by these statutes are acts

which to me are repugnant. I suppose there are many things that I do, not necessarily included in the above list, which are repugnant to lots of people, but I hope no one proposes legislation against them.

The enormous amount of activity demanded by all elements of the criminal justice system, police, courts, and corrections, to enforce laws against such behavior seriously undermines the system's effectiveness in protecting us against those "Index" crimes which make our streets so very unsafe. There are two basic ways in which the so called "victimless" crimes erode the effectiveness of the criminal justice system.

First, these occupy an enormous amount of the system's resources. The Uniform Crime Reports (1970) indicate that 49% of all criminal arrests that year were for "victimless" crimes while only 19% were for the "Index" crimes — murder, rape, robbery, assault, burglary, larceny, and auto theft. Over 500,000 arrests were for drunkenness alone. Pity the poor beleaguered police departments who ride the treadmill arresting millions of drunks, pimps, and two-bit gamblers while 80% of all major crimes remain unsolved. I've been meeting lately with 15 police chiefs of America's major cities and they, if I interpret them right, feel that they have much more important things to do. So with the courts. Anyone who has sat in a night court in one of our metropolitan areas will feel the mockery which courts, congested with such offenders, make of American justice. Because it is in these courts that the poor, the black, the Spanish-speaking, and the troubled experience justice, it is little wonder that they so often hold it in disdain. And the jails. If our jails were relieved of the burden of confining just the alcoholics and the vagrants, we would suddenly have our crowded cellblocks reduced to less than 50% occupancy. We probably wouldn't have to build any more in this century.

The presence of these crimes in our criminal codes erodes our criminal justice system in a second way. It contributes to the system's corruption. Prostitution flourishes because some men want that kind of sex. Gambling flourishes because people want to gamble. And so it is with the rest of the morality crimes. The numbers writer, the prostitute, the abortionist, the drug salesman all provide services which are eagerly sought. They are all willing to pay the police, the prosecutors, and the courts for the protection they need to do business. To them such payoffs are legitimate to the cost of operations. The public corruption originating with these purveyors of vice is a far greater threat to America than are the vices which they sell.

Norval Morris and Gordon Hawkins, two professors at the University of Chicago's Law School, have written a very insightful little book entitled *The Honest Politician's Guide to Crime Control*. They observe:

In this country we have a highly moralistic criminal law and a long tradition of using it as an instrument for coercing men toward virtue. It is a singularly inept instrument for that purpose. It is also an unduly costly one both in terms of harm done and in terms of the neglect of the proper task of law enforcement. . . . It is based on an exaggerated conception of the capacity of the criminal law to influence men. We incur enormous collateral disadvantage costs for that exaggeration and we overload our criminal justice system to a degree which renders it grossly defective as a means of protection in the areas where we really need protection—from violence, incursions into our homes, and depredations of our property.

A revision of the criminal code is, in my opinion, the *sine qua non*, for increasing both the effectiveness of the criminal justice system and the protection which it offers against street crime. An intelligent process of "decriminalization" will relieve our jails and prisons of the nuisance offenders who annoy us and fill some of them with the predatory criminals who threaten our safety.

Reducing the Jail Population

The local jail is the most inexcusable part of our entire criminal justice system. It is a garbage can. It receives that residue for which society has provided no intelligent solutions. The confined group is not a small residue—a tiny fraction of the American public. Each year a number estimated to be between three and four million Americans are admitted to the country's approximately 4,000 local jails. A census of jail populations taken on March 15, 1970, revealed that 160,863 persons were confined on that typical day. Who are these people? Why are they there?

They are mostly people accused of minor offenses—motor vehicle, vagrancy, disorderly conduct, drunk and disorderly, gambling, AWOL, prostitution, petty thefts, and assaults. Many (on the day of the census, 7,800) are juveniles. Others are not criminals at all but persons who are being held pending hearings to determine their sanity. Some are material witnesses. The jail also holds alleged felons—persons who are accused of having committed serious crimes—but these are a minority of the total jail population. In almost every case, people in jail have one thing in common. They are very poor.

We have noted early in this book that the jail as a detention center has only one legitimate function—to insure a person's appearance for trial. The principal method, other than jail, for insuring appearance is the bail bond, which is simply a money guarantee that the individual will show for trial. If he doesn't, he, or the bondsman, forfeits money. Because the poor do not have either the money or the credit to obtain bail, they languish in jail. The moneyed, the organized criminal, the person with friends, does not await trial in jail. The poor and friendless do. Recently, following a riot in a Philadelphia jail, I researched the persons being held. Over 300 men were in that jail on the day of the riot because they could not raise $50 to obtain bond on bail of $500 or less. They were locked up in one of the most miserable of all places because they could not produce $50.

Surprisingly, making bail or not making bail has very little to do with the seriousness of the offenses alleged to have been committed. In our studies, The American Foundation has noted that the person least likely to make bail is the common drunk. In one recent survey that we made in Florida, we learned that only 57% of those arrested for drunkenness made bail while 83% of those alleged to have committed felonies against person made bail. This I am told is fairly typical nationwide. Apparently the drunk is more likely to be a poor credit risk than is the alleged armed robber. Bail is nothing but a credit transaction.

All over this nation jails are bursting at the seams, and sheriffs and wardens are demanding additions to, or replacements of, their crowded prisons. This pressure should be passionately resisted by the public and governing bodies for at least two reasons. The jail is destructive to the human personality and should, therefore, be used only as a very, very last resort. Secondly, jail is a very expensive and counterproductive way to deal with the problem of crime. As we traveled the country, we saw alternatives evolving which appear to be more civilized and less destructive. More importantly, they are in keeping with our basic constitutional presumption—that a person is innocent until found guilty.

Bail Reform

Largely as the result of the significant work of the Vera Foundation of New York, new alternatives for traditional bail bonds are developing and being used successfully in many places throughout the United States. There are several varieties of alternatives which I have observed personally.

The first is release on recognizance or nominal bail. At the place of first hearing, usually a magistrate or police court, but sometimes in the intake section of the jail, skilled interviewers question the arrested person using proven questions and rating scales. The purpose is to determine the accused's stability—his likelihood of appearing for trial without the imposition of either jail or bond. If one scores sufficiently high on the rating scale, he is released without bail or with nominal bail—often less than $10.

In other jurisdictions, government itself has entered the bail bond business substituting a public program for the private—and frequently corrupt—bail bond system. Under this system, the accused applies to a public bonding agency for bond. Usually he is required to pay the traditional percentage as a deposit—generally 10%. Thus if the magistrate has placed the bail at $5,000, for example, the accused must place $500 as a deposit. A major advantage of this public system over the private one is that on appearance for trial the accused receives almost all his deposit back. In the private system, frequently the deposit is the bondsman's fee.

A third type of bail reform is the community bail program. I have been interested in two community bail programs, one in Bucks County, Pennsylvania, where I live, and the other in Philadelphia, where I work. In both of these places, public spirited individuals and organizations, such as churches, have pledged their real estate and other holdings as guarantees thus enabling them to "go the bond" of very poor or unstable people who could not, in any other way, meet either the cash or the stability requirements of bail bond or release on recognizance.

Another pioneer and successful pretrial release project is operating in Des Moines, Iowa, where skilled staff interview defendants who have been unable to raise bail. The interview is brief, concentrating on the defendant's social, criminal, and employment histories, and his current friends, residence, and job. The information is checked after which the staff makes what is largely a subjective decision to accept or not accept the client for pretrial supervision. If the defendant is accepted, an effort is made to assess and meet his needs and to encourage him to develop stable community ties. And, of course, he is supervised.

Many benefits are very evident to date. For one thing, the project is practically paying for itself. The expenditures for the project in 1971 were nearly $144,000 while governmental savings realized were $135,000. The project saved 3,343 defendant jail days, including 1,231 days that would have been served by defendants who ultimately were not found guilty in trial.

The project also saved hundreds of thousands of dollars in capital construction expenses. In Iowa, the state had condemned the Polk County Jail which in August, 1970, was reeling with an average daily prison population of 130, consisting mostly of pretrial detainees. But in 1972, thanks largely to this project, the jail population was down to 75. The jail has regained state approval and a new prison is no longer necessary.

Diversions by Police Agencies The Law Enforcement Assistance Administration, through the state planning agencies, has financed several worthwhile programs which divert large numbers of persons from the degrading jail experience.

In Erie, Pennsylvania, for example, we visited a relatively new city jail that was, on the day of our visit, empty. It is almost always that way. In fact, four of the five cellblocks are being used to store things—not people. This fundamental change has occurred because the Erie police have intelligently decided that alcoholics don't have to be dried out in a jail cell. A program called "Operation Crossroads" has replaced the jail as the community's response to the street drunk.

Crossroads is a storefront, a van, and people—many of whom are reformed alcoholics. When the police receive a call that a person has had too much to drink, they don't send a squad car. Rather they call Crossroads which dispatches its van. The skilled staff may take the intoxicated person home if he is sober enough to know where home is. If he isn't, he is taken to the storefront to sober up. If need be, he may stay at Crossroads for several days. Should prolonged residence be desired, he will be taken to a large old residence operated by the organization.

Similar diversionary programs are evolving which use the social agencies of our communities to divert (and even begin the process of helping) the transient, vagrant, drug abuser, and those troubled with domestic problems. This kind of diversion at the police level brings the police into more positive relationships with the community. It affirms an important notion—that police are capable and desirous of determining that specified classes of persons should not be considered criminal, should not be arrested or incarcerated, but should be considered persons in need of medical and social assistance.

Another diversionary technique at the police level worthy of special note is one originated by District Attorney Arlen Specter in Philadelphia. Using "Safe Streets" money from the Governor's Justice Commission, he has placed assistant district attorneys in the police stations to examine, at the time of arrest, the nature of the evidence. If the evidence, in the opinion of the assistant district attorney, has been illegally obtained or is not sufficient to stand up, he will order the person released. Through this method, the prosecuting agency has become a vital instrument to guarantee protection against illegal arrests and seizures and the subsequent horrors of unjustified confinement.

One of the major reasons for the overcrowding of our jails is the overcrowding of our courts. It is not only the increased number of defendants that is slowing up the criminal justice system. It is also the increased demands placed upon the system in the interest of equal protection under the law. These now burden the system so much that, in some places, it is crumbling. In criminal cases, perfunctory handling is becoming much more infrequent. Official after official indicates that recent decisions of the United States Supreme Court have added enormous burdens to the criminal justice system. They say, moreover, that decisions like Miranda, Escebedo, Gideon, and Gault have created infinitely more work for the prosecutor, the police, and the court. As one official said to me, more in truth than in jest, "It is getting

Speeding Up Court Procedures

just as difficult to try a poor man as a rich man." In our view, this is America coming of age.

Recently I took an in-depth look at the criminal justice process in one typical medium-size county. There criminal arraignments were usually scheduled within two weeks. At that time, the defendant entered a plea. If he pled guilty, he might be sentenced right then and there if his crime was a misdemeanor. If he was accused of a felony, he would probably be returned to jail during the conduction of a presentence investigation by agents of the probation department. Approximately two weeks later, the presentence investigation would be received and the man would be sentenced.

If, however, the defendant pled not guilty and asked for a trial before the court, he would wait approximately six weeks until trial. If he chose to plead not guilty and asked for a jury trial, he would not be scheduled for approximately six months. In April the court clerk was scheduling jury trials for late October.

These delays, which have been continuously lengthening over the past five or six years, brought that county jail to a point of chaos.

For example, in 1965 only 13 prisoners had been held longer than 60 days in that jail pending trial. In 1971, the year of our study, 42 had been held for over 60 days. In terms of cell occupancy, this meant that 1,327 cell-occupancy days had been required in 1965 to hold those waiting over 60 days for trial. In 1971 over 3,100 cell-occupancy days (some persons had not yet been to trial, so the exact cell-occupancy total is unknown) had already been required for that portion of the jail population. In that county, as in most which have similar problems, the cry goes out for a new and bigger jail. The solution, it seems to me, is not in bricks and mortar but rather in the diversions and alternatives, which I have already described, and in the speeding up of the court process.

Officials responsible for making appropriations to all elements of the criminal justice system simply must recognize this new fact of life. The prosecutor must have more investigators to obtain the facts necessary to a conviction. He must also have additional assistant prosecuting attorneys to handle the increased number of trials. There must be additional public defenders and their required staff. The courts themselves must have more presentence investigators, more stenographers, more bailiffs, more courtrooms, and more judges to handle the greater case loads and the increasingly complicated steps in the court process from arraignment to sentence.

Expensive as this may be, it is cheaper than building and operating more jails. It is also more humane. And most importantly it complies with our constitutional requirement of the right to speedy trial. It has long been an axiom that prompt justice is the best justice. Experts contend that the criminal justice system provides deterrence only when justice is quick. Prompt justice is becoming more and more rare throughout the nation.

The Jail That We Do Build

We have already discussed the age and intolerable conditions of our jails. In our view most of them violate every value—constitutional or cultural—of our society. They are throwbacks to a less civilized era. It would be easy for me, therefore, to propose a huge new construction program. Anyone who wished could probably demonstrate that America needs a massive jail construction program. If we were to replace all jails (and I am not including state and federal correctional facilities) that are aged, inadequate, unsanitary, unsafe, or fail to provide minimum constitutional safeguards, the construction costs would, in my estimation, exceed $6 billion. No wonder architects and hardware manufacturers all over the country are eager to get into the correctional construction business.

It is our view, however, that this nation should choose not to build more jails until we have made significant commitments to diversions and alternatives including, but not limited to, those which we have described earlier. Then, and only then, should we begin constructing. But unless these program techniques are more successful than I can envision in my wildest dreams, or unless in our great creativity we invent a substitute for confinement some day, we will have to construct new jails. What we now have is an unconscionable blot on our greatness as a people. I urge that we live with what we have *as bad as they are* at least until 1978. During the moratorium we should pour our energy and resources into developing diversions and alternatives.

The new jail that we do, one day, construct will have to be a revolutionary departure from what now exists. The following will be its minimum requirements.

It will have to be located so as to develop, maintain, and strengthen the alleged offender's ties with the community and therefore be convenient to work, school, family, recreation, and community activities. It will provide easy access to the courts, legal services, and to the medical and social agencies. It must be planned so as to expedite the interaction between the resources of the community rather than impeding such activity.

Its design must maximize the positive aspects of human relationships—inmates with family, inmates with inmates, inmates with staff, and staff with staff—while minimizing the dangerous, degrading, and destructive aspects of interpersonal contact. The "cage" and "closed" aspects of security must be eliminated. Environmental conditions comparable to normal living must be created with inmates housed in small clusters of individual rooms void of closed circuit television and other surveillance devices. To accomplish these goals, the jail itself will have to be quite small with a capacity not greater than 300 in the most populous counties.

One basic truth should permeate every design feature. It is that, in America, a man or woman is presumed to be innocent until he has been found to be guilty. As hackneyed as that phrase may sound, the fact is this: no jail, new or old, that we have seen fulfills that basic requirement, even minimally.

Alternatives After Sentencing   The National Institute of Law Enforcement and Criminal Justice, a research arm of the Law Enforcement Assistance Administration of the United States Department of Justice, has been collecting and evaluating techniques being used around the country as alternatives to incarceration. One outcome has been the identification of bold new programs which implement innovative, community-based treatment and rehabilitation. These alternatives are intended to supplement and, in most cases replace the traditional institutional programs. The emphasis of the institute, to date, has been on the young. This has been in order to minimize the penetration of the youthful offenders into the criminal justice system. The alternatives to incarceration programs which the institute has thus far evaluated are applicable, however, with variations to adult as well as youthful offenders.

A wide range of programs has been identified by the institute. Three of them will be described here:

Specialized Intensive Supervision Units Operating Under Probation and/or Parole Agencies. Certain serious offenders have been shown to be amenable to intensive supervision in the community under the aegis of probation and parole departments. The operating hypothesis is that the need for institutional incarceration can be reduced by intensively increasing the degree and type of supervision within the community. Supplemental treatment methods often include intensive individual counseling, group and family counseling, use of out-of-home foster and group home placements, and a range of activity group and work group techniques.

Nonresidential Intensive Treatment Facilities. These nonresidential programs are typically operated by public and/or private organizations. They provide a kind of intensive daytime program which offers special services in-house, such as vocational training, remedial education, or home economics training. The principal feature of the nonresidential intensive program lies in the close staff-client ratio and the availability of skilled, professional services to meet the special needs of youths. Large numbers of nonresidential programs have adopted the guided-group-interaction technique or other intensive group psychotherapeutic orientations as the principal treatment approach.

Foster Home and Residential Treatment Facilities. A number of foster home and residential group home placements have developed for providing alternative programs for serious youthful offenders. The foster home concept is well-known. The group home typically offers a small-scale residential housing unit owned or rented by licensed or authorized agencies or groups. The staff is employed on a contractual basis. Treatment programs vary, but often adopt the intensive group therapy techniques associated with the nonresidential facilities described above. The development of a strong *esprit de corps* in the residential group facility is conducive to peer group control and the development of self-reliance.

In Florida, for example, we saw a network of regional community-based constellations developing which are designed, in large measure, to replace the congregate training schools. I say constellations because in each region there is evolving a variety of state-operated noncongregate programs including probation, after-care, foster homes, small group residences, and community-based residential treatment centers. Several such centers have already been established. The one at Tallahassee called Criswell House was the first and is the prototype for the others, so I shall describe it.

It is a white, nondescript, but not unpleasant structure, located in the midst of a group of young pines immediately adjacent to the municipal airport. About the only physical features it offers are comfortable bedrooms, a kitchen-dining room, and a lounge which doubles as a room for group discussions, which are, at Criswell, the heart of the change process. In short, Criswell House is a very modest and inexpensive residence for up to 32 youths.

For schooling, the youths go to the public school. For church, they go to community churches. For recreation, they use the Y's, the movies, the parks, and the pools which other young people use. For health care, they visit the local doctors, dentists, and hospitals. When they date, they date in town. Those few lads who do not attend school have employment in town.

All this, it seems to me, establishes a realistic environment for personal growth—and equally important—for appraising personal growth. Observers of the correctional scene have long questioned the prevalent practice of measuring a person's readiness for release by evaluating his adjustment to the unreal institutional world. At Criswell, the ever-present effort is toward testing the reality of one's progress against the real world.

Probation and Parole

Probation and parole—supervision of offenders on the streets—remains one of the most widely used and in many jurisdictions the most effective alternative to incarceration. Yet both are very poorly supported in most jurisdictions of the United States.

As a result of a very highly developed probation and parole system, the state of Wisconsin has been able to keep 90% of its felony offenders out of prison. Yet its crime rate remains a relatively low 1,750 per 100,000 compared to a national index of 2,907 per 100,000. Wisconsin's crime index incidentally is far below most states which lean heavily on confinement while using probation and parole sparingly. We know that many factors other than the relative use of probation and parole influence crime rates. We nevertheless think it significant that Wisconsin, a state that treats most of its criminals on the street, has a crime rate far below the national average.

Subsidy Programs

California, until recently, has depended very heavily on commitments to institutions as the principal sentencing disposition. A very rapidly growing state with an expanding crime rate, California, was building or planning to build a new institution each year. By the middle of the 1960's, it was approaching a prison and training school population of 40,000—over twice that of any other state.

It had to stop building and it did by creating a subsidy system. The state paid each county for every juvenile or adult offender that it did not commit to state institutions. The counties in turn developed better probation and after-care services, group homes, and a variety of other alternatives and diversions. The result has been a sharp reversal in the commitment rate to all state institutions—juvenile and adult. The building program came to a halt. We visited, for example, a youth complex at Stockton which was originally conceived as a 12-unit constellation. Each unit was to house approximately 400 youths. Construction was halted after the third 400-bed unit had been built. There are no current plans to build the other nine. At any moment, therefore, 3,600 youngsters will *not* be confined behind the double cyclone fences of that complex. This has been replicated for the adult offender. California, rather than building new prisons, is closing old ones.

Massachusetts has utilized a combination of these concepts to close its juvenile institutions. Other major states such as New York and Pennsylvania are dramatically reducing the juvenile and youthful populations in their traditional training schools. The reason for this initiative lies not in "do goodism." Rather it lies in a pragmatism which is causing America to move toward more productive solutions to the crime problem.

We visited several states in which traditional congregate institutions were so obsolete and overcrowded that immediate remedies were demanded. Yet funds were not available to build additional correctional facilities. The result was the adoption of a much less expensive solution, the prerelease center, which is one variety of the community correctional center.

The term "community correctional center," we have learned as we traveled this country, means different things to different people. We have heard it used synonomously with the field services—probation and parole. In that context, a community correctional center is a storefront where selected case loads of offenders come—perhaps daily or weekly—for intensified probation and parole services. Similarly, operators of halfway houses often call their facilities community correctional centers. Recently, many sheriffs and jail wardens have begun to use the term "community centers" to describe their facilities. Though there is little that is good to be said about typical American jails, most of them are located in or near sizable towns or cities. With the passage of legislation permitting prerelease programs, they can therefore be utilized for work release, educational release, and other community oriented programs. In some places the term "jail" has been officially changed to "community correctional center."

Just as the phrase "community correctional center" seems to have a variety of meanings, so does the word "community." In Vermont, for example, we visited community correctional centers that served three or four counties. They were, in fact, regional facilities, and their communities were, in actuality, a mix of farms, very small cities, and mountain hamlets. In Philadelphia, on the other hand, we saw a community correctional center in a downtown YMCA that drew most of its residents from within a radius of two or three miles. Moreover we visited "communities" which rejected with finality any intrusion by a correctional facility or service into their midsts, while others not only welcomed, but initiated and participated in such programs. In a land as broad and diverse as the United States there is already, and there will continue to be, a great variety of programs answering to the name "community corrections." In my view, this kind of pluralism can be valuable. But it can also become a kind of self-deception. That self-deception, common to corrections, is this—we add a new wrinkle to an old counterproductive program, give it a new name, and then like the alchemists of old, pretend that we have turned lead into gold. We will not turn the lead of our retributive, control-ridden jails and prisons into gold by giving them a new name. Rather community corrections must, in essence, be different from that which has preceded it. And it can be.

I say this because the other human services have already taken paths away from dependence upon congregate institutionalization, and the results have been completely new

Prerelease Centers

methods of treatment in the community. The almshouses of old have been replaced by family assistance, the workhouses by employment insurance, the orphanages by foster homes and programs of assistance to families with dependent children, and the colonies for the retarded by daycare and sheltered workshops. Drugs have made obsolete the dismal epileptic facilities and the tuberculosis sanitariums of yesteryear, and the asylums are rapidly yielding to day hospitals and community mental health approaches.

All of these human services changed because congregate institutions proved to be unsuccessful, expensive, and counterproductive responses to specific human service problems. Change came about also because treatment methods were redefined and the congregate institution became largely obsolete. Treatment in the natural community setting became feasible. And so it will be with corrections. A beginning has already been made.

In Vermont we saw a different variety of community correctional centers which, it seems to us, represents basic changes in the system. The state has taken over the 13 county jails, closed most of them, and created out of the remaining a new community correctional program. These jails still house the untried. They still hold a few misdemeanants serving short sentences, but whole sections have been converted to serve as prerelease centers. Men approaching eligibility for parole or nearing the expiration of their penitentiary sentences are transferred to them from the 162-year-old state prison.

These jails are totally unequipped for any meaningful program and therefore the communities themselves are called upon to provide the missing elements. Men who have been defined as felons work, play, worship, study, and perform a variety of other activities in the community. In sequence they receive day passes, then weekend passes, then brief furloughs, and finally renewable furloughs, during which time they live at home with their relatives and loved ones. All this before parole. In Vermont, the locale for much of the period under sentence has moved from the central prison to the community correctional center, and hence to the community itself. It has become a continuum for testing oneself, failing, testing oneself again— all under the eye, and with the concern and help, of the correctional staff. In that setting a parole recommendation has meaning. The whole program is too new for final judgment, but it is being measured.

South Carolina has been a front-runner in the development of community prerelease centers. That state's early commitment to this type of program grew out of a series of circumstances. It had an ancient, horrible, and overcrowded central prison, not much cash to build new prisons, and remarkably good correctional leadership. The first community prerelease center was established in 1964 at Columbia, the state capital. The old, abandoned, women's prison was converted to this new purpose. From the physical point of view it is nothing much to talk about. The old prison hardware, however, has been torn out and most of the security areas converted into paneled offices for the counselors. The campus is wide open with men strolling around the acres, tossing frisbees and footballs, shooting baskets, playing horseshoes, or lounging in the sun. It should be noted our visit was on a Saturday and men were not at their places of employment.

Since 1964 several additional centers have been opened and still more are planned, so that one will be available for each geographical region of the state. One of the more recent ones, opened in December of 1970, is the Coastal Community Pre-Release Center at Charleston. This is the first center in that state designed expressly for the function it serves. The center is a "Butler" type prefabricated structure with a brick facade. It is located in an industrial area of metropolitan Charleston, very accessible to employment and public transportation. It is designed to accommodate 64 persons.

The plant is simple, yet attractive. One end is for activities and includes a kitchen, attractive dining room, a living room which is probably too small, a reception area, offices for the superintendent and his assistant, and a classroom. The other part of the building is the sleeping area. It contains 32 cubicles, each designed for two men. Each contains two beds, two comfortable chairs, two steel lockers, and a large desk intended for the use of both men. Rooms are decorated to the tastes of the occupants and many contain televisions, radios, and record players. There is a small library. Except for these dayroom-type activities and a small hard-top basketball court, there are no provisions for recreation built into the center. Rather, the men are given passes to enable them to utilize the resources of the greater Charleston community.

The essentials of the community prerelease programs in South Carolina are these. All inmates in the South Carolina state system, except those convicted for serious sex crimes and those whose offenses are of such great notoriety as to bring grave embarrassment to the program, are sent to one of the several centers 30 days prior to release. This is to permit a period of "depressurizing." During the 30-day period the prisoner lives under relaxed circumstances, takes trips into the community, has visits under agreeable conditions, and receives instruction from citizens of the surrounding area on such diverse subjects as job finding, using social agencies, credit and purchasing, health resources, family relations, and motor vehicle operation. In addition, the facilities serve a work release function. In South Carolina one becomes eligible for work release one year prior to parole eligibility. Men participating in this program are found jobs in a variety of enterprises and are paid the prevailing wages.

South Carolina officials are carefully evaluating the results of this program, and as of today their findings seem encouraging. Even if there should be no marked reduction in recidivism the program will have succeeded, it seems to us, in at least three respects. It is more civilized than the congregate prisons; it is less expensive; and it brings the offender and his community closer together. Our traditional correctional institutions too often are merely places where offenders are "out of sight, out of mind."

In Oregon we visited two interesting community-based prerelease centers. One, for men, is located in Milwaukie, an industrial town that is part of the greater Portland area. No one with whom we talked was pleased with the location, but apparently it was the best obtainable considering the opposition of community groups to having community centers for convicts located in their neighborhoods. Transportation to and from downtown Portland is tedious, and the center is not particularly accessible to the work, school, and recreational resources which its residents must utilize.

There is a temporary quality about this prerelease center because the facility consists primarily of a series of large trailers that have been assembled. Two of these trailers are used for dormitories with each accommodating 20 to 25 men. They occupy double-deck beds. It must be added that the crowded condition of these trailers does not seem critical because the men spend so much time away from the compound. Another trailer serves as a dayroom while a fourth provides the food service facilities.

Men are assigned to the prerelease center on a voluntary basis and usually begin their residence there six months before parole eligibility. About 75% of the residents work in the community with the rest involved in either education or vocational training. About three-quarters of the men originate in the Portland area, thus providing continuity of program and opportunity for home visits. Passes are made available and weekend furloughs are allowed.

The Women's Work Release Center in Portland has a very normal and homelike quality. It is a large white house in a changing neighborhood that is probably ideal for the purpose. The area includes larger homes, apartment houses, and some businesses. Transportation is convenient. The house and its grounds are well-kept, and have no identifying markings. This is the residence for 12 women who have been transferred prior to parole from the Oregon Women's Correctional Center in Salem.

There is nothing special about the inside of the house. Its furniture is comfortable, plain, and apparently hand-me-downs. The bedrooms are fairly crowded. Most probably there are not enough bathrooms for the number of women who live there, but to talk to the residents one would think they are in Camelot. We spent a late afternoon and evening chatting with the "girls." No staff person joined us, purposely. The girls did the selling quite eloquently. They were the most enthusiastic 12 women inmates I ever met.

The program is either work or school. One mature woman is studying at the local community college. Most of the others work in nursing homes where help is very hard to get. They earn the going rate, which is low, but they consider the helping of old, sick people an important activity. Of

their earnings they pay $3.00 per week board and are allowed to retain $30 per month for pocket money. The rest goes into their account but part may be used for extraordinary expenses such as the purchase of clothes or the needs of their families.

In addition to work and/or school the women use the community for their medical, religious, recreational, and social requirements. A counselor may authorize two-hour passes without prior application. Absences for 4 and 12 hours must be requested of the director a day in advance. Passes for longer periods require the joint approval of the director and the superintendent of the Women's Correctional Center.

We had earlier that day visited the Women's Correctional Center at Salem, and it seemed to us to be a repressive place. (We are told that the leadership at Salem has since changed.) Yet here at Portland women who, mere days or weeks earlier, had been confined behind concertinas of barbed wire and who hated and resisted every minute, were now working with unparalleled enthusiasm in a totally accepting setting. They, and their director, insist that there is not a women behind those concertinas of Salem who couldn't be treated likewise. Much of the apparent success of this community-based program has to be attributed to a most re-remarkable woman, Elizabeth Worthington, who directs it with patience, faith, and quiet affection.

At University Park, the home of Pennsylvania State University, we studied the previously mentioned exciting education release program called "Project New View." This is a program in which inmates from the Rockview State Penitentiary attend classes at the state university, thus bringing truth to the old chestnut, "I graduated from Penn State not the State Pen." The participating students live in a large brick building near campus. It is similar to the town's many fraternity houses. Each man has his own room—paneled, carpeted, and overall looking like a "typical student's room." We saw a wealth of posters, books, and musical equipment in a state of disorder which probably reflected constant use and enjoyment. The house has two floors, each with four rooms and a kitchen. There is communal cooking, and housekeeping is the required responsibility of the students.

The program is financed jointly by the Governor's Justice Commission and the Office of Economic Opportunity. Each man receives a cash sum plus tuition for each term. Rent is free, but he must budget his money for books, clothing, food, and vacation periods.

So far, staff and resident alike are enthusiastic about this community residential program. It represents a significant step in the institution—halfway house—community residence sequence by which offenders move from total control to free functioning.

The programs of many other correctional institutions now provide for work release and education release programs. Most are very modest in scope involving small numbers of persons. They generally operate out of the main institution without special provisions for the requirements of an activity which takes men through the perimeter security at least twice each day. This piercing of security creates very special problems. Though the men or women who participate in the community program are chosen because of their apparent trustworthiness, they are subjected to most relentless pressures if they spend their nights and weekends back within the main institution. Men who don't have freedom to come and go demand of those who do all manner of contraband. Occasionally, the pressure takes the form of physical threats. "Produce or I'll hand you your head," cannot be taken lightly, if on return from the community a work releasee must eat, sleep, and play in the presence of desperate men. As a result, we saw such contradictions as a person working daily in the free world only to undergo a body search on his return each night. This process was epitomized by the sign on the door just outside the main security grille at the entrance of one institution. Rather than "Welcome," it said, "Strip and Frisk." Such was one's return each evening after a day of responsible citizenship in the community.

To avoid these security conflicts some states have established prerelease centers on the grounds of the main institution but otherwise separate from it. An old farm house serves that purpose at the Rockview State Penitentiary in Pennsylvania while at both Canon City, Colorado, and Hagerstown, Maryland, special prerelease buildings have been built.

The Hagerstown Prerelease Center is a handsome building constructed of the natural stone that abounds in that part of western Maryland. The center is located on the same grounds but several hundred yards away from two larger correctional institutions—the older Maryland Correctional Institution and the new Maryland Correctional Training Center. The grounds around the prerelease unit have been attractively landscaped. The building itself is much more like a motel than a traditional correctional facility. Built in the form of a *V*, each wing provides 25 single rooms which have no security features. The residents have keys to their rooms. At the confluence of the *V* is the public area which includes office space, a comfortably furnished living room, a classroom, and the food service facilities. The dining room doubles as a dayroom. The lack of inside recreation space is a deficiency of this otherwise functional building. There is a delightful little courtyard outside the living room that provides beauty and an element of privacy during visits.

The Colorado Prerelease Center at Canon City is, in many respects, similar to that just described. Like Hagerstown it has been placed on grounds which contain other correctional facilities. In Colorado, the reception center, maximum security prison, medium security correctional center, women's prison, and prerelease center are all located at Canon City. The prerelease unit, like the one at Hagerstown, resembles a motel with four wings off a central rotunda. Two of these wings are for housing, one for indoor recreation and the fourth for food service.

This center has a more limited function than do other prerelease centers that we visited. It is not so much a work release center. Rather it provides a locale for a program of preparole training and indoctrination. Practically all men leaving the Canon City complex move through this depressurizing experience on their way back to the community.

It should be noted that Hagerstown and Canon City are located, like so many of the correctional centers in the United States, far from the major populations of their respective states. This we were told seriously restricts the extent and effectiveness of prerelease and work release programs.

Probably the most elaborate prerelease facilities in the country are those located on the grounds of the Purdy Women's Correctional Center near Tacoma, Washington. It consists of a series of ten apartments. Each of these contains a living room with fireplace, kitchen, dining area, bath, and two bedrooms. The residents have keys to their apartments and, in fact, staff are not encouraged to visit without invitation. Each apartment is most attractively and comfortably furnished. A large common area adjacent to the complex provides ample space for group meetings, conferences, and other prerelease activities. The women residents work in nearby Tacoma and other towns. This remarkable institution is making every conceivable effort to provide a dignified and enriching experience for those persons who are sent there by the courts. Unfortunately its very quality is resulting in a rapidly increasing commitment rate.

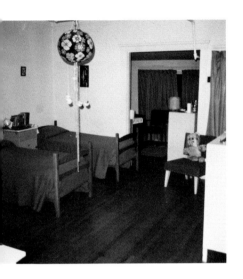

*typical interiors
of prerelease
centers*

Change is the unmistakable hallmark of our times. As I write this section (December 1972) two events, one past and one present, are very much in the news. First, this month is the anniversary of Wilbur and Orville Wright's first flight at Kitty Hawk, North Carolina. That historic journey was only 120 feet in length. The 747 on which I flew last week has a wingspan longer than that. The second event is the flight to the moon of Apollo 17. Within a traditional lifespan, three score years and ten, man's ability to move through air and space has increased almost infinitely.

Alvin Toffler in his book about change, *Future Shock*, notes that if the last 50,000 years were divided into lifetimes of approximately 62 years each, there have been about 800 such lifetimes. Man has spent 650 of those in caves. Only during the last six lifetimes did masses of men ever see a printed word. Only in the last two has anyone used an electric motor. He adds that the crux of the 800th lifetime, the one in which we live, is that we have set the stage for a completely new society and we are now racing toward it.

In that context it is foolhardy for me to try to describe the correctional institution of the future. It has only been during the last three of man's 800 lifetimes that we have had penitentiaries at all. The earliest of these were built so solidly that many of them still are in use. Correctional programs, for the most of these three lifetimes, have been so unchanging that the old walled bastilles did not really become obsolete until well into this century. In fact there was basically very little difference between the Easterns, Trentons, and Auburns that were built in the first third of the 19th century and those maximum security prisons constructed a lifetime later. Until very recently correctional change has lagged eons behind the lightning alterations which are occurring throughout other sectors of American life.

When we first started this study we had in mind producing a very precise guidebook for correctional architects. We naively viewed corrections as a relatively static art. If we could, in our book, describe the better jails, prisons, and training schools that we saw, we could then help correctional people and architects replicate that which is good and avoid that which is not good. We envisioned our task to be an update of the *Handbook of Correctional Institution Design and Construction* published by the United States Bureau of Prisons in 1949, and its 1960 supplement. This we have not done for two reasons.

Such handbooks tend to freeze architectural and correctional concepts. We saw correctional institutions built in the 1960's and '70's which reflected the thinking of the '40's and '50's as expressed in those two publications. But the urbanization of the nation, the explosion of behavioral knowledge, the racial revolution, the evolving drug culture,

Tomorrow's Correctional Institutions for the Adjudicated Offender

the politicizing of the prison population, the new consciousness about legal and civil rights, and many other dramatic changes all have produced a new set of correctional problems and concepts to which even the new institutions are ill-equipped to handle. This very year we attended the opening of a huge $40 million facility that was first conceived and planned nearly a decade and a half ago and which, today at its grand opening, represents most regressive correctional thinking. Yet there it is, brand new, with all its cells and hardware, ready to swallow up human beings for the next half century at least.

We did not produce a new handbook of contemporary correctional design for a second reason. Most of the institutions which we visited have seemed to us to be grossly ineffective, grossly dehumanizing, and grossly misleading in their appearances. We conclude that they are mostly failures — programmatically and architecturally. Why? The answer is not simple, but in many respects it is related to the special ways in which architecture affects corrections.

Unlike most specifically designed environments, the correctional institution is by program definition a total community — at least insofar as the inmates are concerned. An oppressive factory situation, a crowded submarine, a wretched hovel — all have relief valves for the users — other places for them to go and these to some extent by choice. There is also some choice in selecting and modifying these settings. Not so in corrections. There is not a choice of setting (after the fact) and the setting is total, absolute, comprehensive, immutable.

The impact of this totality is compounded by the durability of the human spirit and the imagination which gives it strength. There is little resignation to the fact of incarceration among prisoners; there is almost always some hope — hope of achieving freedom from the totality, and hope of sustaining the ego in the interim.

What functions poorly in the free world may be inconvenient, uncomfortable, and uneconomic; but what functions poorly inside the prison can be, and frequently is, deadly. A poor light source generates resentment through chronic irritation; a security gate becomes an instrument of repression; a hidden stairwell becomes the setting for rapes and muggings; a long, dank corridor diminishes the aspirations of a new day.

Thus the quality of the prison environment is no casual thing. Free people will avoid a badly designed city park — they will not be traumatized or even intimidated by it. There is no avoiding the harsh realities within the fences, even within the dormitory, or the cellblock. In the free world, the inhabitants of a poorly designed domicile will either change it or they will seek relief elsewhere or they will abandon it. None of these can be done within most—

almost all—of the facilities we have seen. We have no desire, therefore, to contribute to their replication.

There is no doubt that the juvenile institutions which we saw were, on the whole, more pleasant and unrepressive than those for adults. A few of them were even spectacularly beautiful. Nevertheless we are unequivocal in proposing no further construction of institutions for juvenile offenders, and the phased closing of those now in existence. There are many reasons for these recommendations but the fundamental one is this: the research that we have read convinces us of the ineffectiveness of juvenile confinement and, even worse, leads us to conclude that it is more than merely ineffective. It actually contributes to future criminal behavior.

Juvenile Institutions

The most recent evidence that supports this conclusion comes from Marvin Wolfgang, Robert Figlio, and Thorsten Sellin's new book, *Delinquency in a Birth Cohort.*

A birth cohort is a population born in a particular year. Wolfgang, Figlio, and Sellin traced all Philadelphia boys born in 1945 who lived in that city from their 10th to 18th birthdays. The boys were traced through school records, selective service lists, and police records. There were nearly 10,000 youths in the cohort, 35% of whom incurred one or more police contacts during their juvenile years.

A principal finding of this exhaustive study is this:

It appears that the juvenile justice system has been able to isolate the hard-core offender farily well. Unfortunately, the product of this encounter with sanctioning authorities is far from desirable. Not only do a greater number of those who receive punitive treatment (institutionalization, fine, or probation) continue to violate the law, but they also commit more serious crimes with greater rapidity than those who experience a less constraining contact with the judicial and correctional systems. Thus, we must conclude that the juvenile justice system, at its best, has no effect on the subsequent behavior of adolescent boys and, at its worst, has a deleterious effect on future behavior.

The primary purpose to be served in dealing with juveniles is their habilitation and integration. These purposes have not and cannot be served satisfactorily by commitment to congregate correctional institutions. Such practice should be stopped as indeed it is being stopped in Massachusetts and in other jurisdictions.

Every planning office, correctional agency, juvenile court, and legislature in the nation should be equipped with automated red lights which flash furiously every time a frustrated public official suggests the construction of a new juvenile correctional facility of any kind. The rites which initiate youngsters officially into the awful world of retributive justice should be delayed long, long past puberty.

Institutions for Women

Women for years have held a favored, and at the same time, unfavored position in the correctional process. It has been favored inasmuch as women are not, in comparison with men, committed to jails and prisons in anywhere near the same proportions. In regard to most crimes—prostitution being the major exception—a series of selection processes at moments of arrest, first hearing, trial, and sentencing sift women out of the criminal justice process. America's state and federal institutions hold only 1 woman for every 34 men who were confined during 1970.

Women who do get committed to institutions most often receive unfavored treatment during their confinement. To a great degree, this is the result of the small numbers who are confined. In a typical jail there will be, at any moment, only a handful of females. Thus, programs are seldom developed for them. Only one matron will ordinarily be on duty at any time. As a result, flexibility in activities is impossible. Even more than men, women in jail just vegetate. This problem of smallness plagues the typical state prison for women also. Most such correctional institutions in the United States confine, at any moment, less than 100 persons and many less than 50. The provision of comprehensive work, treatment, and recreational programs, in such small facilities, is next to impossible except at a per capita, per diem cost that is, in most jurisdictions, prohibitive.

The feminist movement and other changes in our culture may alter all this. As women rightly demand equality in social, cultural, and economic pursuits, the special status which they have traditionally held in the criminal justice system will undoubtedly change. Moreover, the liberated woman may follow the already liberated man into greater criminal activity. Crime statistics suggest that this trend is already well under way. The 1971 *Uniform Crime Reports*, for example, show an 83% increase in the number of arrests for major crimes committed by men between 1960 and 1971. During the same period there has been a 219% increase in arrests for major crimes committed by women. The nature of the crimes in which women are being involved has also changed. Arrests for prostitution, for example, has increased only 87% while robbery by women (traditionally a masculine offense) has grown a staggering 227%. In 1960 only 2 arrests in 17 included women. In 1971, 2 out of every 9 persons arrested were female.

The rate of commitment of women to prison still, however, remains relatively small. We would recommend that it remain that way, and that the state and federal government move toward a further reduction in the population of females in prison. The legislature of my own state, Pennsylvania, has recently passed a community corrections act for women which would remove almost all of its female prisoners from jails and correctional institutions and place them in alternative programs, including small group homes, in several communities. That represents the direction this nation should take during the remainder of the century.

We would enjoin, therefore, against the construction of any new congregate facilities for women offenders even in those states where conditions for women are less than standard. One of the greatest pressures against confinement of women is public and judicial dissatisfaction with many existing facilities. The commitment rate, therefore, remains low. The opening of a bright, attractive, new plant always results in a relaxation in judicial inhibitions against confinement, and the commitment rate soars. It is our view, reached only after thoughtful and painful observations, that confinement, even in the Taj Mahal, is counterproductive. Any step that might lead to an increased use of imprisonment, however well-intentioned, should be resisted.

We present one case in point. Probably the best institution that we visited in America was the new, handsome one, the Purdy Treatment Center for Women, at Gig Harbor, Washington. In our view, both its architecture and its leadership are inspired. Before it was opened, however, only 69 women were imprisoned in the state of Washington. In less than two years of its opening, the population at Purdy has soared to 153, very close to its capacity of 170. It is our conviction that most of this increase need not have occurred, and should not have happened.

In the course of a trip not related to our national survey, we saw one institution that, in our opinion, was even better than Purdy. That was the Women's Prison in Venezuela. Located in a semitropical setting profuse with orchids, bougainvillaea, and poinsiana, its buildings and atmosphere came closer to being the noninstitution than any place we have ever visited. Incidentally, mothers keep their children, up to about four years of age, with them. This is the only women's prison in that entire country, and it serves both the pretrial and postconviction functions. In spite of the double role its population, on the day of our visit, was only 168 women plus their 40 children. Venezuela has a population of 12 million. Purdy, in a state with a census of less than 3½ million, has, as we have already noted, a current population of 153 sentenced women.

Throughout this book, we have been less than enthusiastic about the apparent effectiveness of almost all the institutions which we have seen. The evidence seems conclusive on two points at least. The prison is not a satisfactory setting in which to rehabilitate, and, what is worse, it seems to degenerate. The correctional institutions, however, have not been created merely, or even primarily, to serve the prisoner. They have been created to serve society. They do this, supposedly, in three ways:

The Prison for Tomorrow's Adult Male Offenders

(1) *They punish.* This might not be a noble purpose for civilized nations to pursue but that they do is a fact of life. Punishment gives us satisfaction in several ways, chief among which is that it makes us feel good to know that a culprit does not get away with his evil doings. This is especially significant to one who has been victimized. Moreover, punishment is a negative reward for those of us who don't commit crimes.

(2) *They deter.* Obviously prisons don't deter criminals, some of whom have been in our jails and prisons a score or more times. But they do, we suppose, deter the rest of us. A reasonable person certainly doesn't want to go to prison. Crimes, however, are not always the products of reason. One cannot work in a prison as long as I have and not realize this. A fact not generally appreciated is that the very punishment inherent in imprisonment may be a contributing cause to our prisons being full. Many fairly bright offenders whom I have known committed unbelievably stupid crimes. One can only conclude that they wanted to be caught because they needed to be punished. This could be documented with hundreds of "for instances," but that is another book. I mention it only because the threat of punishment deters some of us from criminality while it incites others to become criminals.

(3) *They quarantine.* The prisons do keep the predators out of circulation for a year, or two, or ten, or more. During that period the offender still often commits crimes, but such crimes are not against us. They are against other prisoners, against people whom we pay to guard the prisoners, and against the state itself. The protection which the quarantine function affords us is far from absolute, because its duration is limited. A civilized nation cannot lock a man up forever for stealing a car, for breaking into a service station, or even for robbing a bank. Most judges refuse to impose sentences that are, in their views, excessive for the offense. When such excessive sentences are imposed, they are very often modified by actions of review panels, paroling authorities, or clemency boards. The average time being served is less than three years, and 99% of all sentenced prisoners return to the street.

The protection which quarantine provides is not complete for a second reason. The prison experience frequently corrodes, hardens, and handicaps many offenders, compounding their inabilities and filling them with hate and a desire for retribution. It also provides the less sophisticated with a schooling in crime. The combination of impaired ability to live in a competitive society, hate, and increased criminal sophistication returns many offenders to the community ready to do unlawful things with new skill and vengeance. Framers of public policy must weigh these realities when choosing imprisonment as the basic instrument for the control of crime.

It is our view, already expressed, that the nation's principal commitments during this decade and the rest of this century should be to reducing crime by correcting the crime-producing conditions in our economic and social structures. This we have called a "public health approach." At the same time, the various states should revise their criminal codes by removing from the purviews of their statutes a whole range of behavior which causes injury only to the person so behaving. The states must also organize their criminal justice systems so as to reduce their present fragmentation and accompanying ineffectiveness. Each system should be provided with a total systems planning capacity so that within it rational and integrated decisions might be made.

The states and their counties must concentrate on reducing the populations in their numerous jails by bail reform, release on recognizance programs, and various other pretrial release techniques. And most essentially, they must assist their prosecutors, defense agencies, and courts toward the accomplishment of speedy justice. Upon conviction, a variety of alternatives to confinement must be available to the courts and correctional agencies. These include expanded and improved probation and parole services, nonresidential intensive treatment units, and small group residences to serve both halfway in and halfway out functions. These are things which we have described earlier in this book.

The accomplishment of all these important steps takes precedence, we believe, over the building of new prisons. The correctional monuments that this generation should bequeath to the next should not be Bentham's *Panopticon*, Haviland's Cherry Hill, HOK's Marion, Curtis and Davis' Fox Lake, or even Gruzen's Leesburg. It should be a series of improvements in our society and our criminal justice processes which, in their combined effect, reduce markedly the use of imprisonment in our land. The prison population, I am sure, could thereby be reduced to 30% or 40% of today's census. These should be the priorities for the 1970's for the federal Law Enforcement Assistance Administration, the criminal justice planning agencies, the legislatures of our 50 states, the commissioners of our over 3,000 counties, and the citizens of this nation.

Having said all that, I hate to end this book with a proposal for prison construction, but my myopic vision does not allow me to see any other ultimate solution. Certainly, not even in the bravest of new worlds, will we be free of people who do unpardonable criminal acts. Nor in that brave new world will Americans revert to the wholesale use of corporal and capital punishments. So until we invent an acceptable substitute for prisons in which to hold the relatively small numbers of intractable criminals among us, we will, in time, have to build better facilities. Today's are mostly unacceptable; they are unmanageable; and they are dehumanizing. As a result, they are counterproductive, contributing to crime rather than to its control.

The alternatives which we have already described will divert almost all situational offenders and a majority of the occasional offenders from the prison of tomorrow. Changes to the criminal code will eliminate the gamblers, drug addicts, many nonaggressive sex offenders, and persons who can best be described as public nuisances. The criminals left to inhabit the prison of tomorrow will be of two general kinds.

First there will be the low risk but repeating offenders — the check writers, car larcenists, embezzlers, and common thieves who have made crime their careers. This group will include persons who steal to support drug habits. The second group will be high risk offenders, and will include those persons with a seemingly pathological, but nonpsychotic, need to assault, to rape, to destroy. Among the high risk offenders will be those denizens of the world of organized crime who occasionally get caught and convicted.

These two types will require different kinds of sentences and different kinds of institutions. The first group — those nondangerous but repetitive offenders — should be subject, upon conviction, to sure but short sentences, probably not longer than two years. These sentences should be served in community-based facilities located quite close to their places of residence. The institution of the future for these felons has already been described in at least two places. The 1967 President's Commission on the Administration of Justice has defined it in these terms:

> *The model institution would be relatively small and located as close as possible to the areas from which it draws its inmates, probably in or near a city rather than in a remote location. Architecturally, the model institution would resemble as much as possible a normal residential setting. Rooms, for example, would have doors rather than bars. Inmates would eat at small tables in an informal atmosphere. . . . Education, vocational training, and other such activities would be carried on in the community or would draw into the institution community-based resources. The prototype proposed here . . . would help shift the focus of correctional efforts from temporary banishment of offenders to a carefully devised combination of control and treatment. . . . It would permit institution restraint to be used for as long as necessary and in carefully graduated degrees rather than as a relatively blind and inflexible process.*

It has also been described in an interesting little book called *The Non-Prison* which resulted from a Ford Foundation grant to the American Justice Institute, a California-based study group headed by Richard A. McGee. Mr. McGee is the former administrator of the California Youth and Adult Corrections Agency. That book is available, and we won't describe it at any length other than to say that its proposed model would have the following features:

· *Secure residential facilities for 48 adult male offenders, housed in three self-contained and highly flexible living areas, each designed for 16 persons.*

· *Non-secure accommodations for 15 additional persons in circumstances similar to current halfway house programs.*

· *A location in the heart of the community that supplies the program population.*

· *An appearance more like a motel, apartment house, or commercial building than a detention center.*

· *Office space and other administrative facilities for programming 250 to 300 former residents who live in the community but remain under the program's jurisdiction and return periodically for group meetings and other services.*

· *A fairly extensive community use area, comprising a gym, meeting rooms, outdoor recreational area, and a coffee lounge/snack bar to facilitate the interaction of clients and the community.*

This model coincides very closely with the one proposed by the 1967 President's Commission and is in consonance with the recommendations of the National Advisory Commission on Criminal Justice Standards and Goals (1973).

The institution for the high risk offender will have to be very secure and designed for a maximum degree of control because it will, by definition, be reserved for those felons from whom the community, the staff, and other inmates need protection. These men will serve lengthy sentences. We have studied many architectural drawings and plans for such institutions. The overall plan that we like best is outlined in the Canadian *Report of the Working Group on Federal Maximum Security Institutions Design,* dated November 30, 1971. Details of that plan follow.

Location

Location near major centers is desirable for these reasons:

· *Visiting by relatives of inmates is easier.*

· *Pre-release planning is aided because many of the inmates will probably come from that city and because after-care placement and employment agencies are more accessible.*

· *It is easier to attract and hold competent and racially balanced staff.*

· *The urban setting prevents the staff from becoming ingrown because of opportunities for staff to interact with other experts in their own and related fields.*

· *Part-time professional staff from the community can be more readily utilized.*

· *Community facilities, such as clinics, hospitals, technical schools, universities, and churches may be used for the inmates and the staff.*

· *The prison can be used for field placement of university students, including those in medicine, psychiatry, pedagogy, social work, psychology, law, sociology, theology, architecture, dietary science, and research.*

· *Although land costs may be higher, operating costs are likely to be less.*

Size

An institution for almost 150 inmates represents the maximum number for a viable program. (250 might be more acceptable in the United States.)

· *Living-unit groups of from 10 to 15 would represent the limits acceptable in an institution such as the one envisaged in this report.*

· *A group of this size will permit interaction while at the same time avoiding the over-intensification of relationships.*

· *The negative aspects of the traditional inmate sub-culture may be more hopefully eliminated in groups of this size.*

· *The intimate knowledge of each inmate acquired by an involved staff identified with the living-unit groups should assist improved program implementation.*

· *Security will be enhanced because of the staff's awareness of the characteristics of all inmates.*

Security

There are two aspects to security—dynamic and static.

· *Dynamic security involves the whole institutional program. It presupposes a program based on joint staff-inmate participation extending to all aspects of prison life and an atmosphere that gives the inmates a sense of hope and accomplishment.*

· *Static security involves both the physical restraints built into the institutions and the security routines in effect.*

· *It is proposed that in this institution there be strong perimeter security. That is, the static security measures built into the institution perimeter should make escape most unlikely.*

· *Strong perimeter security is necessary to give the maximum opportunity for positive program. If the perimeter is secure, program activities can be as free as possible.*

· *When inmates are aware that weaknesses in the perimeter security exist, escape plots are constant. Some inmates will spend their energies in planning escape rather than becoming involved in program and will pressure other inmates to participate.*

· *Electronic and similar devices may be useful, but none is sufficiently well developed to remove the need for supplementing static security with direct staff observation.*

· *Within the institution there should be as much freedom as possible, compatible with protecting staff and inmates from violence.*

Living Quarters

· *Each living unit should have equal security features, although these features may not be used in all of them at any given time. Each room should have its own outside window. Solid doors, electrically controlled and with a visibility panel, should be used instead of barred doors. Each living unit should have a common room for discussion, some kinds of recreation, and for dining.*

· *A kitchenette will be needed as well as interviewing rooms for staff use.*

· *Individual rooms where the inmates sleep should also be of maximum security construction. Each room should have its own toilet facilities to reduce traffic outside the rooms at night.*

· *There should be a dissociation unit of six rooms to be used to give an inmate who is out of control a period to cool off. It should be soundproof and should be located near enough to the sick bay so that the same staff can supervise both units.*

Food Service

· *Food should be prepared within the institution, not brought in already prepared. There should be facilities to permit each living-unit group to dine separately in their own living unit or to permit two living-unit groups to eat together or to permit communal dining for the whole population.*

· *Next to the kitchen, there should be a multi-purpose room. This room should have cafeteria facilities, that can be closed off when not in use, to provide for communal dining. It should also have moveable facilities to permit its use as an auditorium.*

Program

· *Academic education should be available to the inmates in accordance with the individual's needs, interests, and capacities. There should be a library available as well as a music appreciation room.*

· *A cultural resource center should contain rooms of varying size suitable for meetings and discussions. One of these rooms should be so constructed that it can either form part of an adjoining chapel or be closed off to form a discussion room. The center should also contain hobby shops.*

· *A meaningful work opportunity should be available, but not all inmates will be involved in the work program. Some will be in an academic program. Time must also be allotted for all inmates to participate in the socialization program and other activities such as recreation.*

· *In addition to the shops in the industrial area, shops should also be attached to some of the living units to be used when groups, for whatever reason, must be isolated.*

· *Space for physical activities must be provided. In addition to a standard size high school gymnasium, this area should provide smaller rooms for weight lifting and gymnastics. There should be seats for those inmates who want to watch sports events.*

· *The recreation yard should be next to the physical education center so toilet and shower facilities can be shared. In addition to facilities for sports activities, there should be a garden area where inmates can sit quietly.*

· *Visiting facilities should be basically a lounge under adequate supervision and control where inmate and visitors can be in physical contact. There should be lunch facilities to be shared by inmates and visitors. There should be an outdoor garden area connected with the visiting lounge. In addition, there should be security visiting booths where inmate and visitor are separated by a security device for those few inmates who are shown to have abused the open visiting privilege.*

I was pleased to be one of the individuals who was invited to consult with the Canadian Working Group which prepared the report from which the preceding recommendations have been extracted. I am also grateful to the Solicitor General of Canada, the Honorable Jean-Pierre Goyer, for his permission to us to use them in this book.

It is our conviction that institutions such as these which I have described will serve two of society's needs—quarantine and deterrence—better than anything we now have. And, I have no doubt, the very fact of confinement will satisfy another of the public's requirements—punishment. We suspect that such institutions may more likely serve a fourth and fifth purpose—rehabilitation and reintegration, but of this we are not at all sure. Their presence, however, will permit us to quarantine the chronic and/or high risk offender thus allowing the increased use of community treatment for the great mass of situational and occasional offenders. In that there is hope.

Appendix

TO THE BUILDERS OF THIS NITEMARE
THOUGH YOU MAY NEVER GET TO READ THESE
WORDS. I PITY YOU; FOR THE CRUELITY OF YOUR
MINDS HAVE DESIGNED THD HELL; IF MEN'S
BUILDINGS ARE A REFLECTION OF WHAT THEY ARE,
THIS ONE PORTRAITS THE UGLINESS OF ALL HUMANITY.

IF ONLY YOU HAD SOME COMPAJ9

Bibliography

Many of the thoughts and observations noted throughout this book are drawn from the general literature on corrections. In addition to the scholarly and academic references which proved so helpful and provocative, much of our thinking was also shaped by more current material emanating from action-oriented committees and organizations. Further, we drew heavily upon a wealth of material furnished by various states, counties, local departments of corrections, and architectural firms.

The following bibliography, while reflecting the above without attempting to be exhaustive, is intended to guide the interested reader to some resource material for further examination of the many questions and issues raised throughout the book.

**Part 1
The Background
of Corrections**

Barnes, Harry Elmer, *The Evolution of Penology in Pennsylvania: A Study in American Social History,* Indianapolis, The Bobbs Merrill Company, 1927.

————, *The Story of Punishment: A Record of Man's Inhumanity to Man,* Montclair, N. J., Patterson Smith Publishing Company, 1972.

Crawford, William, *Report on the Penitentiaries of the United States,* reproduced from the 1835 edition, Montclair, N. J., Patterson Smith Publishing Company, 1969.

de Beaumont, Gustave, and Alexis de Tocqueville, *On the Penitentiary System in the United States and Its Application in France,* Carbondale, Illinois, Southern Illinois University Press, 1964.

Howard, John, *The State of the Prisons,* New York, E. P. Dutton and Company, 1929.

Lewis, W. David, *From Newgate to Dannemora: The Rise of the Penitentiary in New York, 1796-1848,* Ithaca, New York, Cornell University Press, 1965.

Rothman, David J., *The Discovery of the Asylum: Social Order and Disorder in the New Republic,* Boston, Little, Brown and Company, 1971.

Tannenbaum, Frank, *Crime and the Community,* New York, Ginn, 1938.

Teeters, Negley K., *The Cradle of the Penitentiary:*

The Walnut Street Jail at Philadelphia 1773-1835,
Philadelphia, Temple University Press, 1955.

————, *They Were in Prison: A History of the
Pennsylvania Prison Society,* Philadelphia, The
John C. Winston Company, 1937.

Tyler, Alice Felt, *Freedom's Ferment: Phases of
American Social History to 1860,* Minneapolis,
The University of Minnesota Press, 1944.

**Part 2
The State
of the Art**

The American Correctional Association, *Directory
of Correctional Institutions and Agencies of the
United States of America, Canada and Great
Britain,* College Park, Maryland, 1971.

Bagdikian, Ben H., *The Shame of the Prisons,* New
York, Pocket Books, 1972.

Balchen, Bess, "Prisons: The Changing Outside
View of the Inside," *AIA Journal* (September
1971).

Berne, Eric E., *Games People Play,* New York,
Grove Press, 1964.

Clemmer, Donald, *The Prison Community,* Boston,
The Christopher Publishing House, 1940.

Cloward, Richard A., *Theoretical Studies in Social
Organization of the Prison,* New York, Social
Science Research Council, pamphlet #15, 1961.

Conrad, John P., *Crime and Its Correction: An
International Survey of Attitudes and Practices,*
Berkeley, University of California Press, 1967.

Crittenden, Cassetta, Wirum & Cannon/Hellmuth,
Obata and Kassabaum Architects and Planners;
Division of Corrections, State of Alaska; and
Consultants, *South Central Regional Correctional
Institution: Anchorage, Alaska,* a report, no
location or name of publisher given, 1971.

Fader, Daniel N., and Elton McNeil, *Hooked on
Books: Program & Proof,* New York, Berkley
Publishing Corporation, 1968.

Gaylin, Willard, *In the Service of Their Country:
War Resisters in Prison,* New York, The Viking
Press, 1970.

Glasser, William, *Reality Therapy,* New York,
Harper and Row, Publishers, Inc., 1965.

Goffman, Erving, *Asylums,* New York, Doubleday &
Company, 1961.

Guirey, Srnka, Arnold and Sprinkle, and Hellmuth, Obata and Kassabaum, Architects and Planners; and Department of Corrections, State of Arizona, *Arizona Correctional Training Facility,* a report, no location or name of publisher given, 1971.

Haynes, F. E., "The Sociological Study of the Prison Community," *The Journal of Criminal Law and Criminology,* 39 (Nov.-Dec. 1948).

Martin, John Bartlow, *Break Down the Walls,* New York, Ballantine Books, 1954.

Martinson, Robert, "Prison Reform," *The New Republic* (April 1972).

———— and others, *The Treatment Evaluation Survey,* State of New York, Office of Crime Control Planning, as yet unpublished.

McCorkle, Lloyd, and Richard Korn, "Resocialization Within the Walls," *The Sociology of Punishment and Correction,* edited by Johnston, Savitz, and Wolfgang, New York, John Wiley, 1970.

Quay, H. C., and R. B. Levinson, *The Prediction of the Institutional Adjustment of Four Subgroups of Delinquent Boys,* mimeographed, 1967.

Reimer, Hans, "Socialization in the Prison Community," *Proceedings of the American Prison Association* (1937), 151-155.

Schrag, Clarence, "Leadership Among Prison Inmates," *The Criminal in Confinement,* edited by Wolfgang and Radzinowicz, New York, Basic Books, 1971.

Sykes, Gresham M., *The Society of Captives,* New York, Atheneum, 1969.

United States Bureau of Prisons, *Handbook of Correctional Institution Design and Construction,* Washington, D. C., 1949.

————, *Recent Prison Construction 1950-1960,* Washington, D. C., 1960.

Weber, J. Robert, *Juvenile Institutions Project: Report,* unpublished draft, New York, National Council on Crime and Delinquency and The Osborne Association, 1966.

Wilkins, Leslie, *Evaluation of Penal Measures,* New York, Random House, 1969.

Yale Law Journal, "Constitutional Limitations on the Conditions of Pretrial Detention," Vol. 79 (1970), 941-960.

Part 3
Where Now?

The American Friends Service Committee, *Struggle for Justice: A Report on Crime and Punishment in America,* New York, Hill and Wang, 1971.

Buffalo Law Review, "Prisons on Trial: A Symposium on the Changing Laws of Corrections," Vol. 21, No. 3 (Spring 1972).

Department of the Solicitor General, *Report of the Working Group on Federal Maximum Security Institutions Design,* Ottawa, 1971.

Federal Bureau of Investigation, *Uniform Crime Reports for the United States: 1971,* Washington, D. C., United States Government Printing Office, 1971.

Flynn, Edith E., *Multidisciplinary Research: Sociology and Prison Architecture,* paper given at the American Academy for the Advancement of Science, Washington, D. C., Dec. 1972.

———, "The Special Problems of Female Offenders," *We Hold These Truths,* Williamsburg, Va., 1971.

Hawaii State Law Enforcement and Juvenile Delinquency Planning Agency, *Correctional Master Plan,* Honolulu, 1972.

The Institute for the Study of Crime and Delinquency, *The Non-Prison: A Rational Correctional Program,* Sacramento, 1970.

Kiester, Edwin, *Crimes with No Victims,* New York, Alliance for a Safer New York, 1972.

Law Enforcement Assistance Administration, U. S. Department of Justice, *Planning and Designing for Juvenile Justice,* 1972.

Legislative-Executive Task Force on Reorganization (Corrections), *Toward Reducing Crime in Pennsylvania,* Vol. 1, Harrisburg, Pa. (Sept. 1970).

Massachusetts Correctional Association, *Correctional Reform: Illusion and Reality, Correctional Research,* Bulletin No. 22, Boston (Nov. 1972).

Nagel, William G., "Community Correctional Facilities: Planning, Design, and Construction," *Symposium Proceedings: Community-Based Corrections,* Corrections Division, Institute of Government, University of Georgia, Athens, Ga., Feb. 1972.

National Advisory Commission on Criminal
Justice Standards and Goals, *Report of the Task
Force on Corrections*, working draft, 1973,
especially chapters 10, 12, and 18.

National Conference on Corrections, *We Hold These
Truths*, Williamsburg, Va., 1971.

National Council on Crime and Delinquency, *The
Des Moines Community Corrections Project...An
Alternative to Jailing*, Hackensack, N. J., no date.

New York State Special Committee on Attica,
Attica, New York, Bantam Books, 1972.

Nimmer, Raymond T., *Two Million Unnecessary
Arrests*, Chicago, American Bar Foundation, 1971.

President's Commission on Law Enforcement and
Administration of Justice, *The Challenge of Crime
in a Free Society*, Washington, D. C., Government
Printing Office, 1967.

South Carolina Department of Corrections, *The
Emerging Rights of the Confined*,
Columbia, S. C., 1972.

Toffler, Alvin, *Future Shock*, New York,
Bantam Books, 1971.

United States Department of Justice, Bureau of
Prisons, *National Prisoner Statistics*, No. 47,
Washington, D. C. (April 1972).

Wolfgang, Marvin, Robert M. Figlio, and Thorsten
Sellin, *Delinquency in a Birth Cohort*, Chicago,
The University of Chicago Press, 1972.

About the Author and Team

left to right:
Alfred Gilbert
Jay Friedman
Stanton B. Felzer
Donna Cutler
Norman Johnston,
author of
The Human Cage:
A Brief History
of Prison
Architecture
the companion
volume to
The New Red Barn:
A Critical Look
at the Modern
American Prison
William G. Nagel
not pictured:
Francis Prevost

Photograph by
George Krause

The author of *The New Red Barn,* William G. Nagel, writes about corrections from a unique perspective. For 11 years he worked inside a prison. Much of that time he was deputy superintendent of the New Jersey Correctional Institution at Bordentown and carried major responsibility for classification, treatment, and discipline. After Bordentown he spent four years trying to develop citizen support for improvements to the correctional system. From 1964 through 1969 he served in the office of the governor of Pennsylvania, attempting to coordinate the commonwealth's vast network of human services. Since late in 1969 Mr. Nagel has been Executive Director of The American Foundation, Incorporated, and Director of its Institute of Corrections.

He has served as consultant to the President's Crime Commission (1966-67) and as a member of the Task Force on Corrections of the National Advisory Commission on Criminal Justice Standards and Goals (1972-1973). For this task force he drafted the chapter on major correctional institutions. He is a commissioner on the Governor's Justice Commission in Pennsylvania, a member of the Law Enforcement Council of the National Council on Crime and Delinquency, and a long time participant in the work of the American Correctional Association. Numerous other activities aimed at improving the criminal justice system claim his time and energy.

Romaldo Giurgola, Alfred Gilbert, and Francis Prevost of Mitchell/Giurgola Associates Architects provided architectural consultation and sketches for this multidisciplinary study. Mr. Gilbert traveled with the team and contributed immensely to its understanding of the many physical environments encountered. Mr. Prevost studied the hundreds of architectural plans, blueprints, and photographs, thus contributing toward a more precise understanding of the many correctional designs observed.

Insights into program effectiveness and an analysis of organizational structures were among the many contributions of the team's psychological consultants, Harry J. Woehr and Associates of Philadelphia. The primary representative of that firm was Stanton B. Felzer, Ph.D., whose vast experience in the field of management consultation and in the clinical areas of mental health and corrections brought an unusual sensitivity to a study of institutions. No individual role — from administrator to resident — or pattern of interaction escaped Dr. Felzer's notice. His perceptions of the social environment and observations of staff-inmate relationships provided an understanding of the nonphysical influences which surround the confined.

Jay Friedman, a doctoral student in social work, served the study as its Research Associate. He read widely from correctional literature summarizing for the team's use that which was pertinent. He, like other members of the team, helped in developing the conceptual framework for the study and the outline for the book, in addition to visiting many institutions.

Donna Cutler served as the Staff Assistant for the project and skillfully coordinated and edited reports, data, and the voluminous correspondence which inevitably accompanies an undertaking of this scope. Like every other team member she read each draft critically and suggested improvements.

Other vital secretarial tasks were carried out by Dorothy Welsh and Florence Whiting while Claire Jones diligently handled the myriad of fiscal matters.

Designed by:
Samuel Maitin,
assisted by Deborah Seideman

Printed by:
Consolidated/Drake Press,
Philadelphia, Pa.

Typesetting by:
Graphic Arts
Composition, Inc.

Photographic credits:
Bernie Cleff,
dust jacket,
pages 3, 16, 145 & 146, 197

Martin Dehnel, page 95

Fuccello, page 47 bottom

Harr, Hedrich-Blessing,
pages 59, 65 bottom, 94

U.S.M.C., Air Observation Unit,
page 36 bottom

Hugh N. Stratford,
pages 68, 121 top

Kenneth M. Sturgeon, page 188

All other photographs
by members of the team.

Architectural drawings:
Francis Prevost,
office of Mitchell/Giurgola
Associates Architects,
pages 27, 39, 43, 44, 70, 72, 74, 75

Front end paper is
composed of selections
from actual prison
publications.

Background page 140
from the original in the American
Philosophical Society Library